God's pencil

A COLLECTION OF POEMS

Frances A. Kulik

NFB
BUFFALO, NEW YORK

Printed in The Untited States of America

ISBN: 978-0-9984018-1-2

God's pencil/Kulik-1st ed.

1. Poems. 2. Poetry. 3. Verse.

4. Christian. 5. Kulik

NFB
No Frills Buffalo/Amelia Press
<<<>>>
119 Dorchester Road
Buffalo, New York 14213
For more information please visit
nfbpublishing.com

This book of poems is dedicated to GOD and my only remaining sibling, my brother Daniel R. Kulik, whom I love with all my heart.

God's

pencil

Contents

Preface

After years and years of writing poetry, I finally got what I could find so try to have some of my writing published. Thinking it would be easy, I staled at retyping some of my works. What a mistake, the time that it took me to get all of this together, has cut into so much of my other activities, that there were times, I almost gave up. But then I am not a quitter so every evening I would sit at my computer and attempt to get something done.

Of course I had a lot of setbacks as my old computer decided to die, my old printer had tantrums and I became disgusted and upset. Finally, with a new computer, plus a lot of other things, I got into the swing of it, and got as much as I could typed, or decided, some could be scanned just as they are.

I am eternally grateful for the encouraging words that some of you have given me. I especially must site my friend Anne Fusco for always believing in me and telling me to keep at it. I am also especially happy to have met Tom McDonnell.

I know that some of my poems are either depressing, or silly, but please keep in mind that I have been writing for a long time, through all the growing up periods most people face. What I wrote is what was in my heart at the time. I feel that God was there to try to teach me, with every verse I wrote for him. He was my thought, I was only his pencil.

I must also thank Father Steven Pavignano, O.F.M. for allowing me to use his hand for the cover.

You will notice there is no eraser on the pencil, because GOD doesn't make mistakes.

GOD'S PENCIL

Oh God, How inconceivable

    art thou.

To me give, what I could not

    take.

From me, take, what I could not

    give.

I am God's pencil,

without his guidance this book of

poetry would never have been written.

OVER EIGHTY-TWO

When I am over eighty two, and living life holds nothing new,

I'll just sit back and think of you.

I'll think of what a thrill to find, our spirits were a kindred kind.

And what a golden tongue, so glib, with lovely words could so

entwine.

To make it now comply with mine.

I'll chuckle in a knowing way, and all the youngsters there will say;

"what makes her smile and act that way." but only I will know.

That once when we were more than friends, you gave me love,

with no pretense, or promise at our own expense.

We knew twas just a phase. That lasted way too short awhile

which left behind a warming smile,

But oh, what fun and laughter met, so sweet I shall not long forget.

So you will be my memory to keep me still in sanity,

in hope I live to eighty three.

INTERPRETATION

To admit to yourself
     you love
          is a revelation.

To admit to someone else
     you love
          is a commitment.

TWENTY ONE

Twenty one, It must be fun to reach that great old age.

And yet, it must be strange to look behind that certain stage.

Little girl in pigtails, with dollies, playing house;

Calling us and feeling like a very little mouse.

Growing up, and liking it, and going on through school.

Little spats and arguments, but friendship was the rule.

Parties, dances, boyfriends, scouts, happy times untold.

Yet all this leads to just one thought, my dear, we're growing old.

Written for my best friend Natalie P. a long time ago.

I Have Seen Love

I have seen love,
        I have walked hand in hand with it
I have laughed gaily into its face,
        and knelt humbly before it.
I have shared its moments of sweet abandon,
        and cowered in its strong passion.
I have know its bravest moment, and
        felt its weakest sigh.
I have captured it in song, in poetry,
        and in a memory that lives forever.

I have felt love,
        in its constant musings of my heart,
        and repelled it when it sought it wound.
It surrounds and fills me,
        and plucks at my weakest moments.
But, alas I have learned to understand...
        and thus, avoid it

BIRTHDAY NOTE TO GEORGE W.

Here's a kinda nifty gifty,

For a guy who's just turned fifty.

So let 's toast him, raise your stein.

Gosh, he still looks thirty nine.

THE OTHER SIDE OF FORTY

You'd be surprised how young forty looks,

    when you're on the other side of it.

ACTING FOOLISHLY

I was content, my heart was free, I had no troubles
bothering me.

I smiled a lot, laughed, that too. Then August 27th I met you.

What have you done to my cool way? Why do my thoughts so
so often stray?

Why do I sigh a lot, and dream, my foolish heart should really scream.

A poets a fool, and that is true. If I weren't a poet what would I do?

How else could I explain to me, why now, I'm acting foolishly?

AGING MEMORY

Please, look beyond the wrinkles, do, and see behind the frown.
Ignore the graying hair, recall the curls that once were brown.

Remember me as once I was, so lovely in your eyes,
As I will also think of you who filled me so with sighs.

For now we've both grown older, how wise we now can be,
Respect replaces passion. We are now, just you and me.

Dwell not on what I have become, but please do not regret
That in our past, I loved you, and that I love you yet.

For who can tell, if years from now a feeble mind may roam.
Unfettered by the whims of time that keeps us safe at home.

Should I forget my memories past, perhaps you'll come to me
To pat my hand, give me a hug, let me know that you are he,

Who once when we were younger, longed to hold each other tight
and linger over dinner, often talking through the night.

Then perhaps a word or gesture, will give me one more chance
to remember us as sweethearts, maybe just a single glance.

Then just for that small moment you and I will quickly see,
The youthful pair remembered in an aging memory.

AT SIXTY TWO

I remember grass that's verdant green and trees so full
skies can't be seen.

Water in an aqua hue, so you'll see fish swim into view.

A breath of air so fresh and clean, let's you feel exhilarating.

When music had a sweeter tone, one could enjoy it all alone.

No need to amplify the room, to ruin your hearing much too soon.

Nor listening to the screaming vent, in guise of entertain..er ment?

The walk you took was free of fear, no matter if afar or near.

No locks were needed, no one dared to enter what some others shared.

Respect, respect for someone who, would then return respect to you.

Ah, that was time when life was sweeter, folks much nicer, cleaner, neater.

I guess it's all a point of view, but then again, I'm sixty two.

THE AWAKENING
OR
THE LAUGHS ON YOU

When you think you're the special filly

in his corral, and you find your only

one of the herd.

An Added Word

Enclosed, my poetry, old and new,

And prose that tells a tale or two

Some were written long ago,

In moods of happiness and woe.

Some more recent with intent

For friends, in love or fun were sent.

All in all, herein they'll be

A seldom seen.....profile of me.

the author

ALWAYS YOURS

A year ago, my darling, a year ago, today,

you broke my heart in pieces,

and then you went away.

You didn't know you broke it,

you seemed so happy then.

For you had found somebody else,

where I thought I'd have been.

And now a years departed, and though

my dreams are through,

In ashes, little embers still burn,

with thoughts of you.

A Through Z

How come with so much alphabet

B, C, D, E, F, G. H. and I

We had to use three J's a year, January, June and July?

Two A's for August and April, and I shouldn't mention M

March and May are somewhat gray.

Thank God there's just one N.

November, roll it o'er you tongue

It sounds just like it feels

Cold, blustery, expecting snow,

When home and hearth appeals.

What happened to K,   L, O, P, Q, R.

And T,   U,   V is naught.

W,   X,   Y,   Z a hopeless thing

And nowhere to be sought!

At least T and S and W

Were used in weekday names.

But all the rest are made, I'll bet...

For playing spelling games.

AFTER THOUGHTS

It seems that time flies by so fast, when I'm with one I love,

But when he left the moments dragged, like rainy clouds above.

The fun and joy we shared a while, in memory must remain,

Until that longed for moment if we can meet again.

He wandered off, without goodbye, with a sign or word.

And I just sighed, and whispered soft, a wish he never heard.

I wonder should I have said, that I will miss him so?

Should I have kissed him when he left, should I have let him go?

No one can tell what might have been, nor what will be, I know.

But one thing's sure, my love for him, and how I miss him so.

ACCEPTANCE

Mother says "t would be alright, if I can really get you.

And Father gives his blessing, although he's never met you.

Sister says it would be grand to have you as a brother.

But my brother says you're "well, OK" and just like any other.

How presumptuous I must appear, you haven't even tried

To tell me what you feel for me, still I know deep inside

That even though you're unaware, how deeply I love you.

Somehow, I know what's in your heart, and that you love me too.

AND NOBODY KNEW

A long time ago, he made me a bow,
a symbol which said to me.
"I love you" it said, he smiled then he fled
and nobody knew, but me.

A long time ago, he gave me a rose,
and placed it within my hand.
He spoke not a word, so nobody heard,
 but what he was saying was grand.

A long time ago, he looked in my eyes
and longingly kissed my mouth.
And nobody knows, how the thrill of it glows.
That he loved me, there is no doubt.

A long time ago, I gave him my heart,
but sadly we bid adieu.
I loved him you see, but it never could be.
Still, I wonder if ever he knew.

ALONE AT CHRISTMAS

All alone at Christmas

while the world around me cheers,

It's gaiety, it's happiness

just fills my eyes with tears.

My memories though peasant,

remind me of the time,

when I too, sang these happy songs,

when Christmas joy was mine.

I walk along the quiet street

The snowflakes silent trail,

do all they can to cheer me up,

but realize they fail.

For all alone at Christmas

is not the way to be.

Alone, I reach the Holy Crib

then Christmas is with me.

LOVE IN A DIFFERENT WAY

So now the song is at an end,
yet thoughts are still of you.
Who once was sweetheart, now is friend.
When did love say "adieu"?

We shared part of eternity,
Now can we both pretend?
This was a bit of madness,
yes, a game that had to end.

For now remembered yesterdays
the pleasure and the fun.
Can we recall forgotten things,
Is this all that we've won

I promised once, I'd love you more
with every passing day.
And do, in my simplicity,
love in a different way.

FORGOTTEN PAGE

And now, goodbye

    and I will be

        like the last page you have

            just turned........and,

      as quickly forgotten.

      Tomorrow is already there

        in your mind, and

            yesterday.......is gone!

CREATING FOR NOTHINGNESS

What fools are we, who sit in silence, secluded by ourselves to the confines of our small world, while others sit idly by chattering away about nothingness and nonsense. Creating, doing, accomplishing nothing. While we, though no one reads, nor cares what we do, sit by, busily, creating for nothingness.

THE MAN WHO ONCE WAS BOY

The man who once was little boy,
Whom I remember well.

Are all a link to yesterdays,
in thoughts, on which I dwell.

Through sorrows, worries, happy times
we shared each one in part.

Which, altogether, closer bound
us always, heart to heart.

He wandered through my happy life
a child filled with fun.

Inventing games, and building dreams
till now his dreams begun.

Who is this man, who once was boy
whom I hold dear to me?

My dear young brother, now grown tall
and soon a groom to be.

Accepting now, as life may give
each trial, hope and joy.

He stands immense in my esteem.
This man that once was boy.

TO MOTHER

When I was still in heaven, amid the angels fold.

One day the Lord looked down at me, and this

to me he told. "Come child, for it's your turn,

to look o'er all the seas, and choose a Mother

of your choice, whomever you may please."

There were so many in the world, and yet I

could but see, just one, one you, the Mother

meant for me. I chose you 'cause to me, you were,

the best beyond compare. Your smile was sweet, your

way was good, I'd place my life right there. And as

the years have passed, I see, how right the

course I laid, for darling, what a wonderful,

sweet Mother you have made. Today, upon my knees,

I speak, to my Lord on high, GOD bless and keep

my Mother well, and strong as years go by.

Keep her healthy, pretty too, and happy as can be.

And let her know, I love her, Lord, she means the world to me.

BILLET DOUX

My billet doux tho" syrup sweet

is always sent on time.

Yet, never do you praise my notes

At least I write in rhyme.

BIRTHDAY MESSAGES

My friends are like flowers

In my my garden of life.

Where seeing them often,

reduces my strife.

Among all the blossoms

there are but a few

who cheer so completely,

as someone like you.

Happy Birthday

A Birthday verse

If I were a baker,

      I'd bake you a cake,

Or maybe a butcher,

      I'd cut you a steak.

But alas, I'm a poet,

      my joy and my curse,

So, I bid you "best wishes" my own way

      in verse.

BEING IN LOVE

My breath comes in gasps and my eyes refuse to remain open. I sigh deeply and with less effort. I tremble although I am not cold

I feel a blackness closing over me at times, and yet I do not reach the point of fainting. I laugh with much more abandon, and I weep at the slightest provocation. My senses are acute and distinguish his step, his voice, his laugh, out of all the others in a crowd.

I feel his eyes on me when he is across a room and sense the kiss his lips are placing on mine. I want to reach out to him, but find my strength is gone leaving me hopelessly grinning as a Cheshire cat with no thoughts, save one....him.

THE BLIZZARD OF "77

The winds blew hard, the snow fell fast, and motorist were stranded.
To areas of warmth and food, the frozen quickly banded.

The cities blighted areas, for once were nice to view,
Beneath the snowy blanket, every place looked bright and new.

The news spread fast, around the world, that roads and lines were tied.
Had Buffalo slipped into a fault and just as quickly died?

The networks carried stories, we were impressive news
Why, to this day you'll hear some folks still give their varied views.

The first time that disaster folks confronted such a sight.
Where 'er you looked the streets were still and snow fell through the night.

Where does one start, the question was. What do you do with snow?
To clean it up, you need to have somewhere for it to go.

560 Main became our home, through long and weary hours.
New friends we made, we were well paid, but time that too, devours.

The blizzard parties have been held, but ours should be unique.
WE cleaned things up.....so raise a glass, say, how about next week?

Of course the folks at FDAA, who live far from out city
and other too, who can't attend, indeed it is a pity.

But we can drink their health and feast and talk of better times.
We'll meet together on the tenth, of course at Valentines.

BE THANKFUL

The time that God has given us, is not for useless waste.

Nor is it just for working, in hard or hurried haste.

But to enjoy the world, It's Spring and Winter, too.

To be appreciated, all, and loved each day anew.

Nor is it made for idling, to wait for fortunes breeze.

Or looking to the other man, to buy your daily ease.

No grumble not of weather and storms do not erase.

Just take a look around you, let smiles alight your face.

Behold the sunlit mornings, that brighten everyplace.

And see the beauty of the land, when rain has washed its face.

And climb the hill, and say a prayer, and ever thankful be.

That God has given you the world, and in it set you free.

VALENTINES DAY VERSES

Cupid shot an arrow,
but, 'cause I'm not as handy.
I'll wish you happy Valentines day,
and say it with some candy.

- - -

Valentines day has come and gone,
and not even one man sent
A token, small, a loving note,
and never a penny spent.

Perhaps cupids arrow missed its aim
else he needs his bow re strung.
It's a sorry day to face alone, unclaimed,
unloved, unsung.

- - -

Perhaps I was the Valentine who scorned you long ago.
Alas, that seems unlikely, cause I'd love you for a beau.
So just in case you don't receive, at least one Valentine.
Let this be just a token, love, to make up for lost time.

BROKEN HEARTS

There must be a place where GOD alone

keeps safe for broken hearts.

Where all the tears we shed each day

are held to mend the parts.

So someday at a future time,

perhaps, again I'll see.

My broken heart, repaired and glued

to love, when it's set free.

ONE AND TWENTY

When I was one and twenty, astute and fancy free,

the lads of one and twenty, had no appeal for me.

When I was one and twenty, I scoffed at warnings said.

That if I stay too picky, I'd sleep, alone, in bed.

So now, I'm over thirty, ten years have long since flown.

If there are single lads around, they're hiding or unknown.

I should have heeded what was said? Or maybe there may be,

Someone who's left still looking, and pickier than me.

LIFE'S LADDER

When dreams lead us onward,
    then time is a thief.

So comforting friendships,
    are often times brief.

Thus talent that's warming,
    refreshing and bright,

is many times thwarted and lost
    from our sight.

Here's hope that your ladder
    is steady and strong.

Each rung holds you firmly
    to bear you along.

Where ever you wander
    you surely will lead.

For folks touched with magic
    are sure to succeed.

I Wish I Were a Sailboat

I wish I were a sailboat, sailing out across the sea.
With someone at the tiller, who is very fond of me.
With a cloudless sky and day that's dry and a breeze
       that comforts me.
I wish I were a sailboat, sailing out across the sea.

I wish I were a sailboat cutting swiftly through the wave,
Fierce winds that drive me onward, through a storm I have
       to brave.
With the wind and gales blowing cross my sails,
      and a flag that's waving free.
I wish I were a sailboat, sailing out across the sea.

I wish I were a sailboat tossing gently on the crest,
competing in a Summer race, knowing I will do my best.
With a gallant crew that will see me through any storm
       befalling me.
I wish I were a sailboat, sailing out across the sea.

I LOVE YOU

I love you – In every little thing you do,
      In every way you want me to   - I love you.

I love you - With every moment you're away
      My love will grow in every way - I love you.

I love you - In times of happiness or woe
      When I am feeling sad or low - I love you.

I love you - With each new phrase you say to me
      I love you more emphatically - I love you.

I love you - Beyond all thought of earthly din,
      If but one kiss from you I win - I love you.

I love you - And yet in time if we must part
      You'll always stay within my heart - I love you.

HEARTS BE BOUND

Would that I could, compose a verse

       that binds your soul to mine.

A lingering tie, one end to hold

       where thoughts could thus combine.

Where you, could then the other keep,

       and like a ribbon round.

Our thoughts could pass from one to one

       Within our hearts be bound.

MET AND KISSED

Oh, Let me feel they warming breath

      thy lips which guileless plea.

When I, at last surrender thus

      and raise my lips to thee.

No promise do I offer thee,

      nor, from thee one insist.

We love for but a moment,

      when two lips have met and kissed.

GUESS WHO

I hope I don't produce ennui
       when e'er you have a thought of me.

Or my lack of laboriousness with
       nose is others' business's.

Perhaps my charm has lost its glow
       or tattle tongue has grown too slow,

and bored your ears with tales so dull
       their presence did, to sleep, you lull.

To lose a friendship, I would hate
       if any I have lost of late.

Thus, do I now, in sonnet grieve
       I've missed you, and your joie de vivre'.

Though everyone their cross must bear,
       to you whose heart is filled with care.

I'll not repeat, I shan't add mine,
       and so this missal I won't sign.

It's just to let know I care
       and in this moments time to spare,

A note, I thought, to write to you,
       put into verse …...by me......

              Guess who?

LOVE

What is it that they say of love, can it be felt or seen?

Is it a spoken word, a thought, or just a magic thing?

Does it combine with other forms or lovely, stand apart?

A feeling of the senses, or a longing in the heart?

Is it complete when souls entwine? Can it be freely spent?

Or is it lasting only when to one alone, it's meant?

Oh, what is love, a lust for life a torrid passion spree?

This pleasant momentary thing beget infirmity.

Where does it start, and to what end? When torment lays its jowls

To satisfy its beastly thirst in anger than it howls.

Why was it set upon this earth, to havoc leave this pair

Who hunger with each passing hour and curse the love they share.

Ah, what is love, remember this, it's nothing there to waste.

It's wisdom, strength and character, and never done in haste.

It's all a part of living and what a heart can bear.

When with someone so special, this love is what you share.

REFLECTION

My heart lies empty, like an open book,

       unread, unknown, and thus unloved.

If you would just take a moment to scan

       through a chapter, a phrase, or a line,

What would I have you find?

Dreams, hopes, memories or love?

The unknown questions lie as much

       in my eyes, as in yours.

Read, so they may reflect onto me

       What I am and what I am to be.

My sister died on January 21, 1986, I wrote this
on February 6, 1986 after seeing a vision of her just a few
minutes after her death.

LINNY

I caught a glimpse of heaven
      as she scampered up the stair.
my darling youngest sister
      and she didn't seem to care,
that she left the world behind her
      where it filled our hearts with dread
that we would no longer see her
      for my sister, now was dead.
She was only in her thirties
      and as beautiful as light.
With a world of love before her
      seemed that life, now would be right.
But the cancer was much stronger
      leaving nothing but the pain,
as we watched the light go from her
      just the shell would now remain.
For her happy spirit left it
      then I saw her on the stair,
tripping happily to heaven
      she'll be waiting for me there.
As she smiled and waved back at me
      I know she's still alive,
while the memory of this vision
      now can let me heart survive.

A Pox?

A pox you say! A pox?
I'd rather cream and lox.
Or "crazy like a fox".
But ne'er a pox, a pox.

Or what a key unlocks,
a present in a box?
A fancy pair of socks.
But not a pox, a pox.

What kind of pox? "hey Docs?
A small or chicken pox?
If chicken, boy, what lucks.
"ti's nothing but the pox!

Get well soon.

—————————————————————

Written for my niece Amanda 4/15/87

PEACE IN SLEEP

Into my little world I creep,

      waiting for eternal sleep.

Or the pain to soon subside,

      with my love there at my side.

Weep, my heart, for bittersweet,

      is this love that's hidden deep.

Conquer all, Oh! angels blessed

      give my soul eternal rest.

Wrest me from this guileful bower,

      rescue me, for just one hour,

Where pursuing I may go,

      peacefully in dreams that grow.

On awakening, life will be,

      no more a burden onto me.

LET TIME ALLOW

I know my days are numbered
and time is flying by.
But there are, oh so many things
that I have yet to try.
So many places I've not seen
where I would like to go.
So many books I have not read.
and folks I've yet to know.
So do not tell me to slow down
as time will take me there.
When simply walking is a chore
and running I won't dare.
Let me keep moving at my pace
let time allow me more.
So I can squeeze in one more dance,
across a crowded floor.
Perhaps then fate will grant to me
one last thing that I wish;
Someone to hold me very close,
and give me one more kiss. s.

CLOUD FACES

There are faces in the clouds that float across the sky,

from Norse or Greek mythology, ignoring you and I.

and 'oft I've mused "are these just clouds, which on the

winds do ride? Or souls of lonely worriers who in

purgatory hide?" Who with thunderous shouts and

lightening bolts plead "GOD open heavens door, and

cleanse one soul of earthly sin so that it float no more."

For suddenly they'll disappear, these clouds of misty white,

as if they never were at all, to vanish out of sight. Then

sunshine gold comes blinding through, magnificent to see,

as if the golden gates spread wide to set one spirit free.

THIS, THEN IS LOVE

How my heart swells when I see his eyes resting on me.

How my spirit sings when I hear him speak my name.

How delighted I am when he steps into view.

This, then is love.

 Not the mating of bodies, but the blending of souls,

melting into one another. Without touching, without speaking.

Quiet, gentle, loving, without possession, yet more profound.

Finally feeling the peaceful throbbing of two hearts, now combined.

This, then is love

I sent the following to Johnny Mercer in 1968, after he had sent a very nice note of encouragement after reading some of my words for a song contest. I didn't win the contest though, but it started a new experience for me by corresponding with someone I admired. I still have a Christmas card he sent me with a picture of his wife and himself.

MY NOTE TO JOHNNY MERCER

Across three thousand miles came a missive

      penned by you.

With verse with which the Lords own son, this

      talent did imbue.

To spark my helplessness aloft, and urge me not

      to quail.

An omen, sir, that's what you gave, so now I dare

      not fail.

In gratitude, thus I respond, In triumph, you I hail.

MEMORY

The echoes fade and time goes by

      forever in my heart a sigh.....

A whisper now, goodbye, goodbye.

Yet ever in my memory

      a thought will bring you back to me.

Then I will cry for days now flown,

      to realize I'm all alone.

Again, in time, I'll heal, and then,

      a new song brings you back again.

To start the circle all anew,

      with all the things we used to do

And echoes of a distant day

      rekindle memories to play.

Then when the song is finally through,

      I sigh again, and think of you.

Lyric Lothario

A lingering loneliness leads me to

      listlessness. For a long, lost, love lingers,

His lusty laughter lite my life

      His lust for life, looked lawfully lethargic.

Yet, in limpid, loveless, longevity I lyrically

      must not lie, of what

a luxuriate luminary was my lyric Lothario.

FORSAKEN

Hast thou found a fairer damsel

One whose wit is twice as gay?

One who hears the latest gossip,

But a word she will not say.

One who flirts with sheer abandon,

and will tease you with a smile.

Who will lift your heart to singing,

For at least, a little while.

One who'll toss her curls with laughter,

At amusing things you say.

But reverts to silent teardrops,

at the thought you'll go away.

But, perhaps.....I'm still that damsel,

Though forsaken and alone.

For I've not seen you, in days now,

and dear, you do not even phone.

PARTY REGRETS

I really wish I could join in

    and party some with you.

But duties that were unforeseen

    have beckoned me anew.

I'm sorry that I can't be there

    to let you really hear it.

Know this, that I do wish you well

    and join, at least, in spirit.

WARM GREETING

I look not to yesterday,

nor days of the past.

Or what comes tomorrow

how long will it last.

I'll live for the moment,

that moment is here.

When I greet you most warmly

In hope that I cheer.

MY DADDY, MY LOVE

Into a deep dark chamber they placed my love.
away from my sight and touch.
Hidden from earthly view,
this being that I love so much.

They hid him from my sight forevermore,
but, oh the lingering memories are with me, all.
Warm and tender, as only I can recall.

The way he smiled and his eyes would laugh,
and when he'd frown, how he'd wrinkle his brow.
Or when in thought, how he would bite his lip.
Oh Lord, how I would love to see him now.

I cannot believe a pain so gentle, yet so
unfeeling, could be so great.
I know just one sad thing, I want so much
to be with him, and know I am too late.

Too late, my God, to hold his hand again,
or see his smile, hear him, tell him of my love.
Until, at last, in Gods profound mercy
He grants me once again, to hold his hand,
and hear him say my name, as only Daddy can.

He would endearingly call me Babecaw.

ANGRY ANSWER

You can woo the large masses, and make all the passes

but all that amasses is headache and woe.

If you haven't connections, you just get rejections,

and sorry objections that make you feel low.

To be a success you must kiss the right kinds,

pat and assuage both forwards and hinds.

And sad the creator, the soul separator

who writes lovely music and beautiful verse.

A subject for laughter to scorn ever after,

a ridiculed varmint to torment and curse.

And thus be the life that's a songwriters shame.

Where else but at bottom, must I sign my name.

EULOGY FOR A BEARD

To eulogize a suit at best, is height of

madness, put to test.

Though serving you for all those years,

its hardly worth a flow of tears.

I wonder if you'd give such praise

to one who shares your trying days.

Who worries lest it's set afire,

and wishes that you'd change to brier.

But maybe it's not been as long

and this old friendship's not as strong.

Alas, alas 'ti's just as weird

to carry on so, 'bout a beard.

GIFT VERSE FOR ANNIE

While looking through some cards and gifts
I find there are a special few, I know I'll always
        treasure.
Just simple things, from you to me, not costly
but not cheap.
A picture here, a book, a plaque, are things
I'll always keep.
You seemed to find what warms my heart,
what gives my life some meaning.
What helps me through some mundane task,
and lets me do some dreaming.
Yet, I can't think I've done the same
to cheer you in return.
No picture book, no pretty scarf, no candle
you can burn.
So, I decided I would make this vase
that you can treasure.
Then with each flower you place in it,
you'll think of me with pleasure.

Happy Birthday from your sister, Babe

WERE I A POET

Were a poet, I would not measure time

by hours or minutes,

but by beautiful sunsets and morning dew.

The evening star would tell me when to sleep

and the chilling breezes, when to seek shelter.

The melodious music of the birds, would tell me

when to waken.

And the abundance around me would appease

my hunger.

WHEN I LOVED

When I loved, I loved completely.
How I loved, ah, most discretely.
Quietly, yet warm and sweetly.
Only known by thee and me.

Love was good, through every season.
Love was mine, and yet some reason,
call it fate, or was it treason?
Suddenly twas only me.

Years have flown, and with it madness.
dreams are dust, and I in sadness,
welcome warmly stirring gladness,
thinking now of only thee.

Was I wrong, too soon departed,
did I quit before I'd started?
Who can say, who lives downhearted
who can say, but me or thee?

When I love, if love reclaims me,
will it sooth, or further maim me,
unlike thee, forever tame me?
Who can say, if love will be?

THE WIDOW MOON

The moon opens her eyes

and soaks up the sun.

She absorbs the lingering warmth

and radiates the silence of night.

Then she yawns and encircles all

in her spider webbed shroud.

I cannot take credit for this lovely little verse. It was written by my youngest sister, so many years ago. She is gone now, but I submit her poem here, to be enjoyed.

DREAMS

Where else but in dreams

can some folks stay.

When life gives naught

but days of woe, and loneliness

is everywhere.

Where else is there to go?

Where else, but sheltered in a little

world of dreams, and there, will I remain.

NOTES FROM THE MISTY LADY

Waken, oh spirit of the night,

and linger till the morning light.

To cheer my heart, or dry my tear.

Depending on what song I hear.

Then softly will our memory stray

as silently you steal away.

When sunlight brings a new born light,

Till shadows call you back each night.

BK was on the air from 1 AM to 6 AM, so the Misty lady always left a note, which he would read on the air. It was a fun time.

THOUGHTS

What is there a pen can write,

that a mind doesn't first complete?

ODE TO A FOOT

Foot, you distant appendage, so far from my eye and heart.

Yet so important that without you my day would have no start.

Who greets the day on frozen floor to slap me full awake?

Who moves me to the coffee pot and to my shower to take?

Who walked my worries treading back and forth, when I was feeling low?

Or like Terpsichore showed my delight when days were all aglow?

Ah, foot you right and left, are really quite a pair.

You work much harder inch by inch, than anyone can care.

You carry loads or lead the way through every kind of weather.

Enclosed or bare I wonder how you every stay together.

From year to year your faithful strength projects me through each day

Yet I, in essence, never think of how I can repay.

A pedicure perhaps, will do, a soothing balm, a soak?

Too oft forgotten promises, before their even spoke.

So as I gently rest you in some warming ocean sand.

I write this little ode to you, and honor next, my hand.

MEMORY

A dream you had for tomorrow.....

yesterday.

VALENTINE

I know I'll get no valentine,

I haven't got one yet.

t's not that no one loves me,

its just that they forget.

Perhaps Cupid is too old,

and not as strong, you know.

He still can handle arrows,

but can't release his bow.

PICTURE

You put the pictures away, and hide the little

mementos that always brought him to mind.

Then suddenly one day, someone looks like him,

Or you see a picture, and there it is.

All logic is gone, and you cry.

A picture....only that, and I'm crying.

In Between

To love you is forbidden

      to hate you is impossible.

And thus I am caught in the

      limbo, in between.

Between sensibility and desire.

LESS THAN SWEETHEART, MORE THAN FRIEND

You'll always be so dear to me
I hope it will never end.
You're special, warm, important too,
Though less than sweetheart
More than friend.

At times when I'd be feeling blue,
when lonely hours I'd spend.
I found that I could turn to you
Now more than sweetheart,
Less than friend.

And when my troubles bent me low
In tearful words I'd send,
A prayer that you would comfort me
Now less than sweetheart
More than friend

And years have bound us closer still.
No more can we pretend.
We know we're an infinity,
Though less than sweethearts,
Much more than friends.

ANOTHER GOODBYE NOTE

Remember me, who thinks you grand

Remember me, who said " I found a friend

with visions broad, a wandering pensive lad."

Remember me, who wish you well,

All gladness can unfold.

For you, and all your family,

with happiness untold.

Remember me, who writes in verse,

Thinks kindly of this man.

Remember me, for I shall you.

Good luck, adieu .... Miss Fran

RESPONSIBILITY

R   recognize the fact that you must live your life by rules.

E   enjoy life without relying solely on

S   ex, and do know the consequences of it.

P   repare for the reality of life's tasks.

O   rganize your life so you know how to control it.

N   o one is your keeper or your provider.

S   o

I   nsist on being self reliant.

B   y knowing what you are capable of doing.

I   still in others, proof of your reliability.

L   isten closely when someone is speaking or teaching.

I   magine how confident life can be when you are your own boss.

T   hink before you speak, and especially before you do anything.

Y   ou are the best that can be. If you take on responsibility.

SEALS A MEMORY

If God had only wanted sunshine,

he would not have sent us rain.

If life was only smiles, then,

how would we know of pain?

So God, in all his wisdom

gives us a gift of choice,

which tweaks us to submission

with a quiet, inner voice.

Which tells the ways of living,

with salve of sympathy,

Which heals in time, the sorrows felt,

and seals a memory.

AN UNSENT LOVE LETTER

Oh my darling, if I could tell you now of
 my undying love for you. What words
would I say?

I must close you out of my mind, as I must
cleanse you from my heart. Life is too short
to waste on untasted wine.

Still I recall the tender touch of your soft lips
on mine. How gentle was each caress, which
still brings the warmth to my cheeks.

How very much I loved you, and a part of me,
yes, even today, my heart loves you still.

LOST IN FANTASY

The gentleman smiles, and his eyes
        speak volumes,
though he does not say a word.

He laughs, and in a sudden moment
        all tension is gone.

Relaxed, I move about in a world
        I do not know.

He moves his hand and stirs the silent world
        to fill it with lingering melody.

I am drawn to him, in spite of my ever
        watchful mind.

Oh, master of my soul, be wiser than I,
        for I am lost in fantasy,

Unwilling to give in to reality,
        Yet. afraid to remain in tender dreams.

SOLITAIRE

I sat myself down to ponder, to let my thoughts,
       and mind to wander.

When suddenly the realization came, that no one
       else would play my game.

I did not belong, I thought, so that is why this
       path I sought.

The world was made for pairs of two, and I,
       alone had lost a shoe.

Yes, I was one glove left not found, one earring,
       slipper, always one.

So that is why I never gain, I guess, alone I must
       remain.

Whatever..........I shall not despair,

I'll think myself.............a "solitaire"

(***Sparkle****** Sparkle***)
   ******   ******

WORTH THE PRICE

If I express my feelings, I fear

I shall be ignored, as before.

If I do not, who will ever know?

Yet, if I do, who will care?

And if I do not, who will give a damn.

If I do, I will momentarily brighten a life.

If I do not, I will curse my silence.

If I do I will warm a heart for a while.

And we will smile.

Is it not worth the price?

WE IN WINTER

Your world and my world though somewhat
    spaced apart.

Are closer through our memories, and feelings
    of the heart.

The times we shared, can't be relived,
    nor ever be the same.

Yet time goes on with quest for life which
    seemingly remain.

What need we now? We don't belong,
    it's left to youth and Spring,

Still, we in Winter, carry on, in spite of
    everything.

TRANQUILITY

Sitting in my cozy cove,

by myself, alas I strove,

to write a sonnet bright and gay

describing such a perfect day.

The air is crisp the sun is warm,

within my heart, a scene I form.

Of endless, wild inviting sea,

and God, I know is watching me.

I'm humbled now, I know what's worth,

a stretch of sky, a touch of earth.

A moment in eternity,

and endless, sweet tranquility.

THOUGHTS OF SPRING

I love the sweet smell of late Spring.

The warm breezes stirring the budding trees.

The aroma of earth when the sun beats hot upon it,

waking the dormant flowers into life.

The scent of clean sheets being hung to dry and

the stir of freshness in a long Winter sealed house.

Spring opens an entirely new life for all,

making little rivulets of our Winter snow bound problems.

Each day captures a new dream, filled with ambitious

thoughts of travel and excitement.

Our burdensome shell of Winter falls and welcomes the

progressive thoughts of Summer.

Suddenly, its great to be alive, to be free, to be a

part of God's plan.

TO MY LOVE

In your eyes, the smile of tenderness that draws

      from my very soul, a peaceful like contentment.

On your lips, the sweet tender beauty, that can be

      captured, only in a gentle kiss.

In your nature, a quality, that sets you apart from

      others.

Not better, not worse, just separate and grand.

In you, the glow of living, that makes me love,

      understand, and honor you.

Oh, my love, to possess your youth and age at once,

      Is what makes life worth living.

WILTED FLOWER

Just one more wilted flower,

     lost in his vast bouquet.

One more wilted flower,

     too oft did I turn him away.

One more useless blossom

     dropped all it's petals and bloom.

another dead useless blossom

     Left to my fate of gloom.

Yet, when a new bud rushes past me,

     for myself, I will not shed tears

I know more faded blossoms will

     be joining us through the years.

Do You?

Do you, in the hush of evening

whisper my name?

If you cared, you would, and I'd

do the sane.

Do you, at the break of dawning,

think first of me?

If you cared, you would, then you'd

know I love thee.

WHO KNOWS?

My virtue, they say, stands in the way, of winning
      a person like you.
Although I agree, some small voice in me, says
      "Maybe this need not be true."

Perhaps it's unique that my purity speak, that my
      ways are as fresh as they be.
For I love you, that's told, and I'm terribly bold, and
      besides that, the good Lord's with me.

What I've learned about you, 'bout your niceties too,
      'bout your tastes and your hobbies and such.
Seems incredibly strange, that the Lord should arrange,
      for a person to suit me so much.

So, I'll write you in rhyme, knowing all of the time, that
      the chances I have are obscure.
But obscurity breeds, such unusual seeds, that my
      wildest dreams can endure.

MESSAGE FROM THE MISTY LADY

I know the gifts for others, are surely more delicious

Like cookies, that they bake you, or other favorite dishes.

My gifts are meant to make you laugh, and not to please

your tongue.

'cause laughter is another things that tends to keep you

young.

Your Misty lady

DESIRES

I am lonely Lord,

     for a face I want to kiss. for a hand I want to hold,

     for a dream that's growing cold.

                  I am lonely.

I am tired Lord,

     for waiting all alone, for someone yet unknown,

     to come to me, and kiss away my blues.

                  I am tired

I am wanting Lord,

     in patience, hope and love, and I look to you above,

      to guide me on my lonely way.

                  I am wanting.

I am hopeful Lord,

that in your kind, good way, you will see me in your light,

and give me hope to fight.

                  I am hopeful.

VENDING MACHINE

Tinkle, tinkle, little nickel,

You've got me in an awful pickle.

 I can't get coffee with poetry honey,

and you've eaten up the last of my money.

5 cents

Jim's Farewell

Dear Jim:

With many thoughts and cheerful words, I bid farewell to you.
To wish you more than happy days than you've so long been through.
So many losses in your life, too much for me to tell
Your patient disposition helped, I'm sure, you bore the burden well.
And now you'll not be all alone, existing in your "cell"
You'll have a new found family, who'll help to keep you well.
I'll miss our daily chattering for hours without end.
As brother in law you've always been a true and loyal friend.
I'll have to find somebody else to beg to share a meal,
Somehow my pleadings always failed, I guess I've no appeal.
Whatever, I will take the loss as this is great it's true,
The nicest thing that there can be, for someone nice like you.

(All those EWTN masses and daily rosaries finally came through for you)

May God Bless you with many more years of health and happiness.

With love from your sister in law

Babe

MORE NOTES FROM THE MISTY LADY

True you had said you would scorn me,
Somehow it seemed like a bribe.
Asking for love thus unspoken,
knowing I wanted to hide.

Should I persist in pursuing,
love that is over and flown?
Or fanning the flame of embers grown cold.
That linger, so sad and alone.

I could cut out my heart, my tongue as well
these hands that write me wrong.
And all, because, for days on end you play
me not one song.

Am I still your Misty Lady?

Have I indeed become a bore, instead of being cheery?
Perhaps I write you, oh so much, which makes it rather dreary.
So I'll behave to be again your mysterious Misty lady
And nothing that I ever say will sound a bit too shady.
Then maybe in a week or two you'll find you're missing me.
While in the meantime, I'll remain a poignant melody.

MORE NOTES FROM THE MISTY LADY

(And when he moved to a new Station, the Misty Lady
followed)

I know that I'm no Brenda Starr,
and you're no Mystery Man.
But now and then you touch me in a
way that no one can.

Some days when things just seem too much,
that's all I have to do.
Is turn my dial to E.C.K.
To find my love anew.

Your Misty lady

To BK

The Misty lady roams no halls, nor haunts no silent room,
Nor waits alone to pounce upon her love, who's lost in tune.

Nay, guard thee well, thy empty walls, but search there, not for me.
For I am here in glorious bloom, when 'ere you fain to see

For tho' I am a misty maid, there's more to me as well.
So warm to touch, or gently kiss. Should I, these things, you tell?

So when the night is warm and damp,and mist begins to rise,
imagine that your misty maid, is there before your eyes.

But not with noise or mournful wails, I'm not a ghost, as yet.
I wait, anticipating more, than songs I can't forget.

Your Misty lady patience bides, for no one know but she.
Her time will come, when she will wrap you in her mystery.

ANSWER TO A CANCELED INVITATION

For just one day, I do suppose

you'll give that day some sweet repose.

Refreshed, you then can get more done,

instead of being on the run.

The second, well, now, let me see

what would I do if it were me?

I'd check my calender to find

the something that I had in mind.

Then with the last, it would be fine,

Who knows, perhaps this could be mine?

Unless, of course, I just can't see

you don't enjoy my company.

Inhale........................... (this is what I would call a pregnant pause)

But, I'm not giving up at all,

I'll make another try.

Perhaps you'll find some time for me,

As soon as late July.

We'll see.

Egotism

Egotism is the sublime opiate that deadens

the pain of mediocrity.

To Overflowing

My heart is empty,

      like an overturned glass.

The longing is here,

      ah, it shall not pass.

Not until I see on his return,

The eyes, the smile,

      for which I yearn.

I'll wait a month, a week, a year.

Then when the glass is filled

      I'll disappear.

BECAUSE OF YOU

My life was full, I thought that sure, and all my sorrow spent.

Then you stepped into my sweet world, and brought me malcontent.

My heaving breast betrayed my sighs, my eyes were in a glaze

Where, once, I heard, folks must ask twice. I'm in a giddy daze.

If this be what I think it is. I must shake loose somehow.

I've gone the route, I won't burn twice, This must end, here and now.

How logical my mind can be, now to convince my heart,

But somehow, it's gained all control, and feels so very smart.

Where can this lead, how will it end, what can I say or do?

My spirit, heart and mind are lost. And all because of you.

THEN WILL I SMILE

Wait till the fire is over, and she no longer beams

Wait till the glow is faded, like awakening from some dreams.

Wait till you're tired of her, and feel compelled to stay.

Then will I smile, ah, shall I smile, and look the other way.

Wait till the sigh of Springtime, takes you longing to the past.

Wait till a tender memory, make you want to hold me fast.

Wait till you're lost without me, make believe that's like before.

Then will I smile, ah,shall I smile, and softly close the door.

UPON THIS DAY

Upon this day, a lass I went
and found to my surprise.
The world an ever changing place,
Yet filled with every guise.
I sought to amble forward through
a life that's good and straight,
Yet stumbled on my lonely road,
to brambles fell, in wait.
Pursuing such an earthly loss
The life I led was spent
In empty, hopeless wastefulness,
and wrought with malcontent.
Researching then, my only light,
I prayed he set me free.
To fill my heart with hopeful life,
With blessings yet to see.
As thus I came, thus I must go,
A woman worldly wise.
But in my Masters eyes I'll be
A lass, to yet surprise.

TASTY THINKING

To be a poet, you must be cleaver,

with earthly good, your mind must sever.

But poets like me, will profit...never.

I write of food and fellows, fair,

of thick brown steaks, and bright blond hair,

That's why, I won't be worth.....a pare.

Of crispy lettuce, wish I knew,

...ham and eggs, Jim's six foot two.

...coffee, cream; his eyes are blue.

Know another, toast and jam,

Brother's cute, hot roast ham,

Raisin bread, mm, what a man.

Buttered toast, light, hope we meet.

Chicken and dumplings, yet, Bob's so sweet,

Pie a la mode, makes my heart beat.

My minds a jumble of every feast,

that tickles the tongue of manly beast.

The things I should think of, I think of least.

So, now, I'll take leave and repast in peace.

THE BOSS IS AWAY

One day out, well after all

    a man must have a day.

Two days out, he must be ill.

    He'd never stay away.

Three days out, things must be worse.

    Poor thing, laid up so long.

Four days out, it's serious

    I wonder what is wrong?

Five days out, I'm really lost,

    I miss his …. uh   dictation?.

What's that you say, he's out of town,

    He took a weeks vacation??

THANK YOU

A simple phrase, too oft' not said,

to those we walk among.

Thought surely needs repeating

In every kind of tongue.

So here, I've put together,

This very brief oration.

To say just what I want to say,

in words of every nation..........

Bardzo dziekuje	(Polish)
Me dasa pu	(Ghana)
Gracias	(Spanish)
Salmat po	(Philippines)
Tenk ou tumas	(Papua New Guinea)
Teimakasih banyak	(Indonesia)
Spas ibo	(Russian)
Dank a schien	(German)
Go Raibd Maith Abat	(Irish)
Hvala	(Croatian)
USA	(THANK YOU)

CONFUSION

When I smell the grass, that's newly shorn,

See the pale full moon, at evening born.

While the sun sinks low, for a night to rest,

My contentment says I've fulfilled my quest.

Yet

Another me thinks beyond, and back,

and I feel a loss in my one way track.

As my gaze is drawn to the, now full light.

Of a lovely world in the pale moonlight.

Was it once? Is it now? Will it ever be?

Am I...I?   Am I …. who? Was I ever me?

GOODBYE

When I moved beyond your sight
I knew, no longer could I fight.
My aching heart had told me so
That we were worlds apart, I know.

I cry!

Yet, still the memory lingers here,
Of one love who was warm and dear.
As friends we parted, still I pray,
As friends, we'll meet again, someday.

I'll try.

But should our paths ne'er fain to cross, .
You'll live within my heart.
With fondest warmth, but sorrow too,
That we, just had to part.

I sigh.

Go

If I tell you, go, is it not better to have known love

    as a beauteous thing.

Not as an arduous passion, forgotten in haste,

    But to be remembered in love?

So, go,. Do not waste another moment in my web.

    I release you, and forget you.

I erase you from my memory. I tell you, go.

THESE ARE THE WORDS THAT WILL BE CARVED INTO MY GRAVESTONE.

GOD grant to those with time,

more ambition.

And to those with ambition,

more time.

DAMNIT

If I'd never met ya,
I'd never knowed ya.

If I'd never knowed ya,
I'd never loved ya.

If I'd never loved ya,
I'd never missed ya.

But I did,

And I does,

And I do.

Damnit!

FLASHING SCENES

I see before me flashing scenes, of colored hues and endless greens,
Of azure sky 'tween fields and hills,
Near traveled roads, like mureled stills. Of lush green valleys fresh
with dew, and waving grass the winds pursue.
A county lane, a lumber yard, a station master, standing guard.
Thick pine groves that hug the earth, serene brooks babbling,
A new crops birth. Cattails, ferns, a pond, blue green.
It's been a while since these I've seen.
There's a barn that's shabbily clad, a young colt prancing, feeling glad.
Old homes, new homes, billboards, lakes. A Summer camp our train awakes.
A flock of birds in early flight, as on I travel toward the night.
Baseball diamonds, kids at play, there's a farmer, mowing hay.
Long gray bridges, rivers wide, two trains passing side by side.
Old towns, names I'd long forgot, shopping center, parking lot.
Bustling freeways, boats at sail, semis carrying food and mail.
People rushing to and fro, laughing, frowning, on the go.
Brand new buildings being born, out of slums now old and worn..
Fenced in houses, gardens, plots, garbage dumped in hope it rots.
Open space that could give joy, but no jobs near, to folks employ.
Forests towering, mountains high, climbing endless toward the sky.
Through my trip I write and peer, till my destinations near.
Then I recollect my dreams, review, once more, the flashing scenes.

MAY WE NEVER CURSE
WHAT IS OURS IN VERSE

An artist sees what's in his heart,
    a poet what's in his mind.
And strange as it may seem to some,
    we're all alike in kind.
And thus we share our tacit dreams,
    yet wander aimlessly.
Except to some, who cautious, wise
    project their infancy.

As thus, my friend, with you, who
    breathe, a life into a word.
And much as I, we share this grief,
    perhaps, nobody's heard.
Yet we, we, carry through our days
    a gift that binds, it's true.
For poetry, like friendship brings,
    fond memories to you.

FORGIVE ME LOVE

Forgive me love, for lonely is
     my heart.
Each hour that you are away,
     the moment we're apart.
Perhaps I've come to realize
     you mean the world to me.
Perhaps it's strange I'm so consumed'
     with senseless jealousy
I guess I care too much for you,
     or you care no enough.
I'll' try for less possessiveness,
     but dear it will be rough.
I've loved to have you flirt with me,
     and tease, as in times passed.
Your words and actions sang to me,
     I hope this too can last.
We are so much alike somehow,
     in feelings and in thought.
And sorry that I've hurt you so,
     with all the joy you've brought.
Forgive me please, give me your warmth,
     your so unselfish heart.
I, cannot, live, will not exist,
     if we, for long, depart.

THE SONG WRITER

A song, a song, everyone is writing them,

Anyone who holds a pen, and turns a certain phrase

Feels he is now a songwriter

A king on which to gaze.

But, oh, the lowly songwriter,

Who's written songs for years.

Can get to not one publisher,

Then ends her days in tears.

She prays that tends will turn her way,

And music soon will be,

Melodious tunes, with lovely words.

As songs are meant to be.

She will write of love, and beauty

Though she finds right from the start

Her time and talent now must die,

Within her broken heart.

HE WROTE "BUSY"
I REPLIED WITH THE FOLLOWING:

B et I can, a verse compose

U sing the letters you left me.

S o as to prove, I appreciate the fact,

Y ou did not, just, forget me.

I'll Write A Note

"I'll write a note", I said to them,

"to tell hin that I care."

My friends, all taunt and laugh at me,

and say "You wouldn't dare."

"Not only that" say I to them,

"Ill write in verse and rhyme,

 twill only take a moment, though

for him, I'd make the time."

So thus this poem, these lines I write

I'm glad that this could be.

My thoughts are just to say to you,

Thanks for remembering me.

SPECIAL FRIEND

A rare and precious thing, a friend.

A harmony that has no end.

While here among the friends I claim

I happily inscribe your name.

Perhaps the times may change the view,

Our friendship will just take it's cue,

Retiring to a quite spot, but always

there and ne'er forgot.

Then later when I reminisce, my working days

with times like this,

I'll think of you, and understand,

In you I've known a special friend.

SMALL THINGS I AM THANKFUL FOR

Warm sunny days,
Good food to satisfy my appetite
A smile I can display.
Dear loving friends.
But highest in my thankfulness and warmer in my heart,
Is a friend, like you, so dear and sweet,
With whom I hate to part.

** ** ** ** ** **

Friendship is a golden gift, it's special, warm and rare.
How great I've had so many years, this gift, with you to
share.

** ** ** ** ** **

A wealth of treasure, could never buy a friend as dear as
you.

KUDOS AND THANK YOU

Beyond my worldly worth and some

I can't begin to pay,

The debt of gratitude I owe

to you from day to day.

The countless niceties you do,

I'm sure for you, will glean,

A crown in heaven, which will surpass

Any man has ever seen.

MON AMI

You're a charming hostess,

    the evening was great.

That's quire obvious, else we'd not

    stayed that late.

The snacks were delightful, the champagne divine.

    The dinner, delicious, where did you find time.

The things we discussed, were of interest to all

    I even enjoyed that small spat in the hall.

You made us feel welcome,

    Our thanks go to thee.

    Let's do it again.

    We had fun, Mon Ami

I Sent Poems Like These With My Songs to Publishers

Enclosed a song "Twas writ by me". For your perusal

and to see, if just by chance, I've learned to write, the

kind of song, that may be right.

So, listen, please,and let me know, if there's a chance

that it may show, I've just a mite of writer's tact........

If not, well "Hell" just send it back.

ANDY

The day is here when you depart, the hours fly along,
and all I have to keep you near, is an album and a song.
At least this much I have alone, not shared by two or three.
Those many years since first we met, has left it's mark on me.
I cannot tell as hard, I try, what is this charm you hold.
Must be my feeble mind is stumped, or else, I'm getting old.
Oh well, why fight it, it still nice to care for someone who
can sing such lovely melodies, like Gods own chosen few.

Much success in Boston, Andy, and thank you.

7/3/60

How long ago was it, that I would scrawl a verse to you?
How many yeas have past us by, and oh, how quick they flew.
To hear you're now returning, is hard to comprehend.
You knew me once, now try to guess, who greets you here?

A friend

These are notes which I sent to Andy Williams who always
askedme to join him for a while, whenever he was in town.

SLEEPLESSNESS

Last night, I could not sleep, for want of you.

I woke and tossed my torment all about.

Even prayer, could not break through,

the spell that held me fast.

And, if for a moment I did pass on to dreams,

they, which were all of you, woke me with a start.

Only to put me back again, in the web of

sleeplessness.

Silent Love

Perhaps I should shout it from the house tops,

    tell the world and all,

        but I feel I'd rather remain a silent love.

This way you cannot know, that I gave my heart

    to you, the day we met.

I hear your voice, and feel your heart, and

    your nearness to me.

Thus I hold, to myself what we shared for a small while.

LOVE YOU ANEW

I'll ply you with candy,

     martini's and charms

Till you rush to me warmly,

     and rest in my arms.

I'll coax and cajole,

     till I feel when we've kissed,

     that the long months of waiting,

no longer are missed.

     I'll gently caress you,

bestow with each touch,

     a deepening meaning.

of love that is such.

     I'll love you completely

and when I am through,

     start from the beginning,

to love you anew.

SLEEP AND DREAMS

And thus, I fall into beautiful dreams of you,

    where in you hold me close,

    and kiss away my fear.

My troubles disappear,

    as dew upon the morning rose.

My heart is filled with the wonder of you,

    and oh, my love it shows.

On awakening, my happiness bubbles over

    to fill my heart with cheer.

And color my cheek, where you have kissed me,

    where you have held me near.

You brought me joy in dreams,

    yet, when awake, you know me not, it seems.

WITHIN MY MEMORY

Every moment you're away,

    just brings you closer dear.

I miss you, oh so very much,

    I wish that you were here.

I miss the music of your voice

    and miss your gentle smile.

But here within my memory,

    you linger all the while.

TRANSGRESSIONS

And he, in one small passing phrase,
      had all my soul, my heart erased.
For once I loved him hopelessly,
      how hopelessly, I could not see
For though I loved him as my life,,
      I did not know......he had a wife.
Now that I know, my souls at peace,
      his words gave me a quick release.
Although they tore me through and through,
      they cleansed me now, to love anew.
The question is, can I survive?
      How can I keep this heart alive
Still I pursued most rigorously,
      I loved him, oh, so desperately.
And though I loved him, still I know
      It's time, I had to let him go.
For he was never mine to claim,
      although I'll loved him, just the same,
Then years from now when we are old,
      we may recall our love untold.
We'll still remain as soul mates, we,
      this love recall, affectionately.

NO MORE THAN THIS

Too late, the time of stealth is gone,

 yesterdays promise has quickly died.

Thought about commitment hides in the past,

 thus crippling the sight of a future.

Without this, tomorrows dawn is but a vapid dream,

 perhaps a wish we can't redeem.   No more than this.

The love that had so much promise in it's completeness,

 wrong or right, is gone.

Leaving an empty passiveness and a Mona Lisa smile.

QUESTIONS

Why is it, once my heart so light,

    now seems to always shield a fight?

Why is it, I, so warm and bright,

    must always shade my glow, at night.

When I was warm, content and knew

    no one at all, why did I meet you?

You brought me misery untold,

    and took the part of me that's bold,

then wrung me dry, and tossed aside.

    A love gone cold, which I must hide.

If only this could be as true,

    as folks suppose of what I do.

But sad, alas, my heart is free.

    and it loves not, just feeds off me.

The following poem was written because I sent a six foot envelope to Steve Allen. Steve Allen was the host of the late show long before Johnny Carson. He may have been one of the first hosts of the Late Show. He had a great talent, as a musician and comic. His show had some of the great young singers that moved on and succeeded in their own right.. Steve Lawrence was one of his singers, along with Andy Williams, Eydie Gorme and I think Gogi Grant. I don't really recall, as it has been a long, long time. At that time in my life I was very busy with writing songs, both music and lyrices. My one downfall was that I couldn't put my music on paper without someone doing it for me. I paid different people to write out my songs. I would sing them on tape and have them transcribe them to sheet music. Ah, what a changed world it is now.

I would then send my words and music, with a tape to different song publishers, usually in New York City to see if they would give them a listen and perhaps get something published. I though, if I would make this six foot envelope, and have my name and address on the front, when it got on the TV someone would notice and remember that they saw the name on some tape or music. It didn't work.

Steve Allen did put the envelope on screen. He had them put Steve Lawrence into it, and then he turned to the camera, pointing directly into it and said, "Remember Frances A. Kulik, you asked for it." It got a big laugh and applause, but no publisher called I did get a call from a publicist in Chicago, who offered me a job.

Many, many years later, while I was working at radio station WBEN, I met Steve Lawrence in person and told him that I was the one who had sent in the envelope. He gave me a big hug and kiss and told me that I had made his career take off after that show. Nice of me to do that, too bad he didn't sing one of my songs. Oh well. Perhaps God had never meant for me to be a songwriter, only a poet.

The poem is called "Envelopes"

ENVELOPES

This one here, would fit his fingers,

    and the next might fit his hand.

You could cram his head in this one,

    if the strain, he could, but stand.

If you curled his leg up tightly

    You might stuff it into here.

Then this little square one.

    surely it could hold an ear.

But that boy I could not damage,

    so my poem, at once, must cease.

Enclosed you'll find one giant envelope,

    Please send Steve Lawrence, in one piece.

My address, not incognito,

    though it goes by name of Smith,

One, six, five, then is the number

    ??? (there;s no word to rhyme with" ith").

So you send to the right person,

    My name, I'll have to let you know,

Send that cuddlesome, handsome fellow,

    To Baby from Buffalo.

CONTEST VERSE

I will not need one hundred words to say why I love you.

Why one alone would do the job, to say just why I do.

Fantabulous, would say it, your newscast is the best.

In every way that's meaningful, they stand out from the rest.

Irv, Rick and Tom are really pros, in how we want to hear.

The latest news and sports, and what the weather will be here.

Now, as for me, I'm rather neat, and though I'm not "jet set".

I may be just a bit shop worn, but I'm not marked down, yet.

Box Top and Twenty Five Cents

Again I send my quarter fees,

      this time for book of recipes.

Again, I wonder where I fail,

      for recipes, don't come in mail.

Again, I write, and write some more,

      repeat what I said once before

Forget the order for the book,

      Just send some nice young man,

who'll cook.

BRIDE'S REPLY

I vow, this day, to be your bride,

    to live forever by your side.

To do your bidding every day,

    to love, to honor and obey.

I'll try to be a worthy wife,

    to make, for you, a happy life,

and with thr blessing of the Lord,

    keep good my promise, every word.

IF I SHOULD LOVE AGAIN

If I should ever love again,

    as I have loved before,

I wonder who will be the one

    that I will so adore.

I wonder who will be so fair,

    who could replace his way?

Whoever could, in life, compare

    to make the past, passé.

I wonder if I'll change at all,

    or will I feel the same?

Or will we be like strangers,

    if I should love again?

REMINISCENCE

Your smile, like moonlight on the water, gently caressing the waves.
Like the sound of your heart, beating in tune with mine.
The longing to touch you, the yearning to kiss.
The spell of the music? The nearness of you?
Hmm …. I reminisce.

Your eyes, the hidden mockery, behind a lying glow,
You humming, so quietly, that I could only hear.
A sigh in the darkness, You stirring in your chair.
The spell of my perfume? A feeling we share?
Hmm..... I reminisce.

And I, like innocence unaware, blurting forward,
caring not if etiquette was crumbled.
Unaccustomed to such a moment, being something,
I should not be...........myself.
I still reminisce.

Then we, letting the moment pass us by.
Not planning a future meeting,
Leaving that to chance. And in the days that follow,
You regret............and I......
I reminisce.

REMEMBERING YOU

I stand and gaze out at the sea

    the moonlight, my only companion.

I hear a sigh in the darkness,

    and realize, it is mine.

Far off in the distance,

    I see the lights of the city,

and I think of you.

    Knowing that you are not alone.

I turn my back, but my heart remains,

    Unmoved, remembering you.

Till tears blind my eyes,

    and thus, sobs replace the sighs.

HOLY EUCHARIST

The angels guard it for it must,
      by human hands be left, untouched.
Yet, surely you can see the Priest,
      when high he lifts this holy feast.
Alas, but to a human eye
      the Priest is man, not God on high.
For was it not said, once by "HE"
      that you shall "Take the place of me".
to place the host on every tongue,
      the first communion of the young.
That leads them, keeps them on the road,
      to point the way to his abode.
Now think it be so strange and odd,
      That you receive this gift from "God"?
This sacred host, so pure and fresh,
      In truth is Christ, his blood and flesh.
No, ponder not, but bow your head,
      and think of him, when he was dead,
And watch the Priest, you see, it pleases,
      him to try to be like "Jesus:,
Now in its' earthly alter palace,
      He places it, the Blessed chalice.

SUNLIT MORNING

The time that God has given, is not for useless waste.

Nor is it just for working, in hard or hurried haste.

But to enjoy the world around, Its Spring and Winter too,

To be appreciated, all, and loved each day anew.

Nor is it made for idling, to wait for fortunes breeze,

Or looking to another man, to bring your daily ease.

No grumble not of weather, and storms do not erase

Just take a look around and let a smile alight your face.

Behold the sunlit morning, that brightens everyplace,

Observe the beauty of the land, when rain has washed its face.

Then climb the hill and say a prayer, and ever thankful be

That God has given you the world, and in it set you free.

MAGIC OF THE PAST

Now the magic of the evening, was the magic of the past,

and although we tried pretending still we thought it wouldn't last.

For we've searched for love in others, and pretended it was true

that we thought you can't recapture, what was once the love we knew.

Yet somehow the spark within us, seemed to wake a new found theme

when we looked into each others eyes to find a warming dream.

Then in time, a new awakening seemed to wander in and through,

still I wonder could it ever start to build that dream anew.

When I see you once again I hope, I'll see into your heart,

To find a love that has now found, a brand new loving start,

THREE THINGS

Three things a man will never admit.

How many women in his past
.
False teeth.

Thinning hair.

BIRTHDAY NOTES

I tried to make a birthday card

      that would be nice for you.

I then attempted birthday verse,

      but failed in that way too.

So, I just thought I'd try a rhyme,

      to send this thought your way,

I hope you'll have a birthday,

      that is grand in every way.

FOR SOMEONE WHO TURNED 25

Here's five, and five and five and five

and five more wishes too.

Happy Birthday for each new year,

May they all be great for you.

QUOTES.......

As my curiosity dwindled,

my peace of mind increased.

A Thank You Note

Thank you for the pitcher,

    it is such a lovely hue.

I really cannot say enough,

    except, it was sweet of you.

SOLDIER BOY

A soldier boy I can't forget, was one I saw, but never met.

His eyes were dark, his hair was light, and how he sent my heart alight.

It was about two weeks ago, at a parade, I liked him so.

He acted silly, cute and my, he was just anything, but shy.

His pal and buddy, a Marine, was only glanced at, never seen.

He kept on calling for some "Joe", was that his name that I don't know.

Well, that is life and its design, I wish that soldier could be mine.

I found this on a page which indicates it was written sometime in High School first week in November .probably 1946 to 1948

JOHN

A pixie darling, full of fun.
  A sheer delight to see
A man of men, who's young at heart,
  and full of deviltry.
His swaggered step and tossing head,
  shows spirit and conceit,
but how his tender words impart
  a message warm and sweet.
Ah, what delight to be with him,
  from time to time each day,
to share his laughter and his fun.
  each in a different way.
He tempts me with his wistful look,
  cajoles me with his eyes,
and lures me to his open arms,
  while murmuring winning lies.
I try resisting, but I can't,
  I'm caught within his spell.
And with each kiss, I'm tighter bound.
  I'm lost and know it well...

NOT FORGOTTEN

There are times in life when we feel we should call,

Yet, to call, could possibly be an imposition.

So a card, thought, longer in arriving, sometimes does the trick.

Beside, a call lasts only a short time, where a card can be placed

on a table, where it can remind you of the fact that you

are being thought of...

So many words, to say a simple thing.....like

I hope you are recovering, and beginning to feel well.

You are often in my thought, and always in my prayers.

I just wanted you to know you are Not Forgotten.

TO LINDA

Beautiful eyes of heavenly blue,

    hair that shines like sweet golden dew.

A face that all of the angels have kissed.

    Oh I think of the days of love I have missed.

Leaving you behind, while I'm at work or at play.

    Missing the sweet things you do and you say.

Knowing you only when it's time to sleep,

    Remembering to pray, so your health will keep.

Loving you so, you're so sweet, pure and fine,

    Heavens own child, though I claim you as mine.

Mine in a way only true love can show,

    dear, sweet baby sister, I do love you so.

FAREWELL TO BUD

It seems that luck as smiled on you,

    and fate has gaily strung,

Her stars to guide your ladder,

    with success on every rung.

Such is success but sad goodbyes,

    must also be a part.

Our wish to you is most sincere,

    and comes right from the heart.

Good luck, adieu, we'll miss you much,

    Our best each now extends.

Remember us, not just as names,

    But also as your friends.

CONGRATULATIONS

There are some things unmistakable,

like looks and talent true.

So it's really no surprise to hear,

that you are in Who's Who.

I've always said you're quite a lot,

and even more than that.

Congratulations John, it's nice to know

a real aristocrat.

TO A FRIEND

The beauty that is

    in a lovely song,

expressing the feeling,

    that you belong.

The beauty that lives

    till the very end,

Knowing, remembering a

    favored friend.

I'LL MISS YOU

'll miss your charm, your wondrous ways

The magic of your voice

I'll miss the fun we used to share

until I had no choice

I'll miss you as a vocalist,

till missing has no end.

But most of all I'll miss you as

a very special friend.

LITTLE COTERIE

Better late than never, so it's said.

    So now I take my pen in hand,

That's been so full of lead,

    to finally write this thank you note.

I hope it sounds sincere.

To thank you for your effort,

    which so filled my day with cheer

I'm referring to your rushing 'round

    to get a gift for me,

May I therefore make you members

    in my little coterie.

SEASONAL CHANGES

The sound of a tree, bushy and green,
      Rustling leaves, such a beautiful scene
Sunny or cloudy, flowers in rain,
      Children at play for it's spring, once again.
A view of the world through somebody's eyes,
      Sunset or dawn, all sparkling and new.
Bright forsythia glistening with dew.
      Spring leads to summer which soon will appear
Helping us all shed our wintery gear.
      Now is the time to restore wilted dreams,
When warm summer sunshine continually beams.
      Filling the hearts with contentment and praise,
Giving us hope for some much better days.
      Yet, when fall befriends us again, we will say,
The weather is great, at this time of day.
      Then we'll dream of a new year when snow starts to fall.
We must grumble a little, but we know for it's true,
      That spring will return to confront us anew.

ENCOUNTER

He laughs, and in a sudden moment,

    all tension is gone.

He moves his hand, and music fills the air

    with sudden beauty.

I am drawn to him, in spite of my

    ever watchful mind.

Oh master of my soul, be wiser than I

    for I am lost in fantasy.

Unwilling to give in to reality,

    Yet afraid to remain in tender dreams.

While your words entice me to surrender.

    I am yours, until the music stops.

To Peter

As each day goes by, and nights slip quickly on.

I feel, again, so hopelessly, how very much is gone.

I know, I once, for just a while, possessed you love and faith,

Then lost it within a breath of time, left longingly to wait.

I know each moment slipping by, means so much more time gone.

So if by chance we'd meet again we'll know it's all been wrong.

It cannot be that we were meant to always be apart.

Because I feel that I belong, to you, here in my heart.

Whatever reason, I believe, that you once loved me too,

Yet, can it be a wishful thought, at least I know it's true

That I loved you from the time we met, and love you more today

Someday, a long, long time from now, I'll love you still that way.

NOBODY LOVES ME

Nobody loves me, well, some people do.

    My Mother, my sister and my brother too.

But nobody loves me, no one special heart

    beats for me, only, and thinks I'm a part,

a part of a plan that is lovely and fine,

    with me as the other half, a place where I'd shine.

No, nobody loves me, I'm nobody's taste.

    Alone and forgotten, and oh, such a waste.

PAPER VISIT TO MY BEST FRIEND

Dear Ruth McGowen:

Today I thought of you, because I wasn't feeling good,
And suddenly, I thought of how, you feel, and then I under-
stood.
Somehow my God was telling me to send you, now, a line,
Expressing just a simple though to you soon, in time,
Will once again, be well and strong, and like you used to be,
So that our friendship still can grow and go on endlessly.

I realized how much a part of my life you have been.
To share my joys and sorrows to see me lose and win.
The way you'd always cheer me up, when I was feeling low
And come and pay a visit when you'd other ways to go.
I guess, I felt well, guilty, that I haven't paid a call.
To see how you are getting on, some courage to install.

And so I set about to write this little verse to say,
I pray to God's dear Mother, that you are better every day.
I value you as my dear friend, and though it takes me time
I find that I can say my words much better when in rhyme.

Thus ends my paper visit, but if it brings a tear,
'twas meant to give you gladness, hope, and yes, to also cheer.

TO JUDY, MY SISTER-IN-LAW

Your thoughtfulness, and pleasant way,

your tireless efforts too.

Creating lovely dinners

which all reflect on you.

You seem to never tire

of giving others pleasure

Perhaps that's why you are,

to me, an extra special treasure.

As mother, grandma, sister in law

there can be very few.

Who can be crowned, the "Very Best",

my vote is just for you.

LATE FOR WORK

I face into the wind, feeling the breeze comb the waves from my hair.

    The whistling sound, drowning out the hurry in my mind.

I push each step forward, forcing my anger to ebb.

    Unseeing views pass me by, because I am absorbed in thought.

Striving forward, till I arrive at a destination somehow only known

    to that part of me that is still calm and untroubled.

I feel cleansed, as if the heavy laden humidity has washed

    the anquish from my mind.

then enter laughing at the havoc the wind has taken on my being,

    I face again, the beginning of a new day, refreshed, though late.

NICHOLAS

With words of love thou did employ, to try to teach me worldly joy,

Then suddenly, no sound, no word, ne'er pleasant thought, of late, I've heard.

Could be thou car'est not at all, alas, such fate should me befall.

Nay, let me think, thee much do care, and in my presence, do not dare, to

Linger any length of time, for fear, thou then will make me thine.

Or have I wounded thee, by chance, by passing someone else a glance?

Or failed to note a lonely plea, which thou has sent so willingly?

Of stronger fabric I had thought thy wondrous form was surely wrought.

To brazen any company, and not shy, as thou art with me.

To lose they love, though fleetingly, has oh so deeply sorrowed me.

Then just before my missive end, a call from thou my dear, dear friend.

And joy again returns to me, and I'm content that we, are we.

To lead me to this lengthy tale, in hope its message does not fail.

Be with me now and to the end, be with me as a cherished friend.

Although it is they fervent wish I will not offer more than this.

UNREQUITED LOVE

I've run the gauntlet of playing the fool,

    from here to the golden West.

Embarrassed my friends, and the ones that I love

    by my chasing and giving no rest.

By actions uncommon a womanly girl,

    wise, yet unwilling to give.

Mistaking the thoughts in her own empty head

    for the future she wanted to live.

Pretending the dream wasn't only her own,

    yet feeling the pain of the past.

Still knowing the moment of happiness ends,

    and heartaches will live till the last.

Though fool I have been and fool may remain,

    regret I will ever deny.

For moments are memories living so long,

    that embarrassment, soon has to die.

INVITATION TO A SQUARE DANCE

Swing your partner, out to the aisle

Allemande left, I'm sure you will smile.

Do-sci-doe, with your money in hand.

Pay our fee with a right and left grand.

Sashay down to the Golden Nugget Saloon.

Come in style and swing 'neath the moon.

Duck for the oyster, we'll have the clam,

Fresh or broth and a beer too, Ma'am

Gent and Lady, you all come.

We guarantee that we'll all have fun.

TWO LITTLE WORDS

Two simple little words, often spoken absentmindedly

_____

We say "thank you" when someone holds a door for us

When we receive a gift, get change, get our food at a

restaurant (at least I do).

It is a phrase that gets lost in our conversation because it

has become so common, that to say it isn't appreciated

or some think it isn't needed to be used as often.

It is something we have taken for granted for too long.

You perhaps wonder, why the long dissertation on an

expression we use daily.

The reason, is I need to say it today, to you especially,

with the most profound feeling I can muster as this time.

Ahem......THANK YOU!

A Thank You For Mary

The effort and gracious presentation you put into giving me such joy cannot be so easily acknowledged...so I will try to say it in verse.

Dear Mary:

To get my creative juices going takes more time
than it did in the past.

So I waited unhurriedly till they were flowing
and my efforts are starting at last.

I thank you for giving me sweet tears of joy,
with surprise of my music to hear.

Then adding a luncheon, including my friends
just makes you especially dear.

So that's why my thank you has taken this long,
I've been searching for words that will do.

Now, simply, I'll try in my miserable way....here goes....

Thank you

Thank you

THANK YOU1

BIRTHDAY VERSE

Take all the nicest adjectives

    and all the sweetest phrases.

There still would be abundant space

    in which to sing your praises.

It's rare to find a lovely flower

    whose aura never ends.

I'm happy that I'm numbered too,

    among your many friends.

A Christmas Remembrance

Anne & Bill loved Christmas so much they would put up a tree early in December and leave it up till March. They would also entertain guests, at their home, with a very late dinner which lasted for hours. By midnight a king or queen was proclaimed and the festivities continued.

The meal consisted of a French onion soup, and a salad. The highlight of the evening was when a cake was brought in, with coffee. The cake had hidden in it a small trinket. If you were the person to get the trinket, you were crowned, with a real royal type crown, which you wore for the rest of the evening. Such a jolly time was always had by all.

I, wanting to thank them wrote the following.

Words cannot express with worth, all the pleasures wrought

through the moments of contentment, and, of course, your

luscious broth.

Keeping Christmas joy intact, have anxious moments lulled.

Feeling free to breathe a sigh, with good wine that you mulled.

As sweet moments hold, we must, in these most harried days.

Be glad there's hope, with folks like you, to show us pleasant ways.

WANDERING

The lovely earth around me sighs,

    its' magic beauty fills my eyes.

Its' noisy silence fills my ears,

    Its' loveliness moves me to tears.

The winding brooks, the stalwart grass,

    Laugh at me, each time I pass.

The crickets hum a merry song

    To cheer me, as I go along.

Yet, through my wanderings, I can't find.

    The peaceful yearning, held in mind.

WHAT WOULD...

What would the world be like
        without the magic of your smile?
Which captures moments rapturously
        while warming thoughts beguile.

What would an empty day be like
        without one thought of you?
Without the presence of your touch
        what would I ever do?

What would the night be like
        if we had never paused to kiss?
What sweet and lingering torment
        I would never known I'd missed.

What was my life before we met?
        this fact I know is true.
It's now a better place for me,
        the reason lies with you.

Who Loved You Most

Who loved you most, but could not tell
     for fear the dream would end,
     too soon to be a memory,
      a fleeting thought, a friend.

Who loved you most, alas was I,
     with heartfelt love forbear, too oft'
     I longed to hold you close,
     but you were never there.

Who loved you most, you most ignored,
      left me with tears to cry.
     Although I loved you helplessly,
     I did bid you goodbye.

For youth takes precedence,
     when aged yet undefiled
     must be adult in many ways
     and still remain a child.

Who loved you most, and loves you still,
     it's I, oh, you must see
     I love you more with each new day,
     and miss you hopelessly.

ON MEMORIES AND THOUGHTS

Arising early in the morn, my thoughts turn first to you.

I wonder how you are today, I wish I weren't blue.

I wish I didn't miss you so, I wish I'd made you stay.

But wishing is a feeble thing, when you are miles away.

I think of all the happy times, when you were there with me,

The laughs we shared, the songs, the fun. How nice it used to be.

Then going on throughout the day, I do my daily task,

and say "He's doing wonderfully" whenever friends would ask.

Then, I in utter silence wander slowly down the street,

while dreaming of how sweet t'would be, if only we could meet.

Once more to be again with you, and though the time be brief.

To be encircled in your arms, and then just like a thief,

To steal a kiss, a tender kiss, for fear you'd laugh at me.

At how I treasure all these days, till once again I'm free.

Then, only then, when I'm with you, when you're right there in sight

I'll be content to wait for you and dream each lonely night

I Know

I know, the tender feeling that we share

    will be a memory, too soon.

Yet, between us, no bitterness, no pain,

      no regret.

Only an unknown emptiness.

Step lightly, speak soft.

    Do not disturb my dream.

I'll waken without a heart,

    and so will you.   I know.

IF TRULY I LOVED THEE

If truly I loved thee,
      poetry would flow from my pen,
      like the unbridle forces of a roaring river.

Romantic phrase would come to mind
      as quickly as lightning flashes in a
      stormy summer sky.

And through the glow of a midnight moon,
      symphonic music would thrill me with an
      even greater love for thee.

Ah, but poetry does not flow from my pen,
      but dribbles, straining onward, to perchance
      finish a new forgotten phrase.

Thinking, I've forgotten the words,
      and now my ears are deafened by the roar,
      of those you have placed before me.

If truly, I loved thee. Better not to think,
      but to turn, look to the future,
      with wiser, sadder heart, yet lighter step.

I must not let it be known.
      How truly I loved thee.

CONSEQUENCE & HEARTACHE

We, the fools of the world, sit idly by

> watching the destruction of two souls, and do nothing.

We hover in the background, wisely shaking our heads,

> seeing the ultimate end.

And though our souls cry, our lips are sealed in silence,

> recalling our struggling tramping into love.

The long awaited kiss, all too soon forgotten

> by the anguish of tears.

It is better that he, should make the wound,

> and that we, die in sorrow.

Woe to those who love and still do not know its meaning.

> Its consequences, its heartbreak.

MAYBE

Maybe it's because I'm older now,
      and life is not a game.
But real, and sweet and beautiful,
      and mine to call by name.

Or maybe it's because you were
      so different from the start.
So sensible, so extra nice,
      that made me hate to part.

Or maybe it's because I've found
      that love is something new.
Or perhaps the only reason,
      lies entirely with you.

There is one thing I realize,
      I've find you good and fine.
And feel it is a pleasure,
      from this day to call you mine.

GIFT OF GIVING

The gift of giving, is the gift of love

No matter how trivial or small.

Or if you give in great abundance,

or cannot gift at all.

It is like the thought that one who can

May never even try.

And one who hasn't much to share,

will still go out to buy.

The hope is that, because they feel,

and not because they should.

They give a little to show love,

With feelings that are good.

OR SILENT BE

A warming glow stirs deep within

      my heaving breast,

This wondrous being here so

      near my touch.

Can now be music now be laughter,

      but always, oh so much.

I've harried thoughts, to now

      describe my mind.

Is this what love is? Gentle,

      warm and kind?

Is this, this moment, blessed love

      all mine, and shared.

With this, my darling, if we dared?

What say you soul within me?

      Hear me! Tell!

Have I, at last now touched at heaven,

      or a hell?

That such forbidden fruit should fall to me.

Speak now, oh glorious fate,

      or silent be.

WARM DREAMS

To talk to you by candlelight

    across a cozy table.

To hold your hand, and sigh aloud,

    a pity I'm not able.

To find you warm, sincere and sweet,

    in words and well as deeds.

To have you near, so close to me,

    is all my lifes heart needs.

SPEAK SOFTLY LOVE

Speak softly love, and gentle be thy hand,

and let thy whispered word be heard,

then ask me to command.

Speak sweetly love, for magic is the spice,

of words and actions, gentle, soft, and

beautifully "nice".

Be tender love, my heart is at your feet,

and yours, to crush, or gently place in worlds

of rare retreat.

Speak softly love, and say you understand,

then greet me with a warming kiss,

and softly take my hand.

MY DADDY

Daddy, what is there to rhyme?

What is there that words can say, to let you know.

How insignificant and small is a word,

compared to a smile, a hug and a kiss?

I think, in my moments when all my little problems

      weighed so heavily on my back,

He was always there, to help remove the load.

Oh Daddy.....those jealously treasured memories I hold.

Of a little girl being rocked to sleep, to an old familiar tune.

A game of catch with a golf ball, hikes in the woods,

      picking wild strawberries.

Walking arm in arm through the rain in New York city.

Of encouraging words to wisdom, struggle, worry

      and help.

Oh, pick from my treasures, my brightest gem.

And you will find, it is taller that the mountains,

strong as the lightning in a Summer sky,

Wise as the scholars, and good and gentle as a lamb.

And loved more than any one thing on this earth.

      My Daddy.

After A Trying Day

Oh, if not but, for the love of children,

What empty lives some of us old maids would lead.

A small boy throws his young strong arms around my neck,

and presses his chubby cheek again my ear and whispers,

"I love you Aunt Franny" and my heart swells within me.

As the whisper of a small child turns Gods messenger to

cheer me, after a trying day.

TENDER DREAMS

The mind...........

   paints such pretty pictures,

which, the heart............

   believes, it seems.

But, the eyes, all seeing, wise,

   bring us back.......

from tender dreams.

Too Late

Too late.......

       I've lost the golden moment

       once again........

       as suddenly as realization.

Too late........

       I try but naught can ease the

       pain...........I will not try again

       It's much too late.

COFFEE BREAK

A dry, parched, thirsty gal am I

yet forced to bide my time.

This danged machine, devoured my cup

and also stole my dime.

Yes, there was a time when a cup of coffee cost only ten cents

WHEN WE MET

Twas such a hot and misty day, when

first I spoke to you.

When ties were made, that naught can break,

no matter what they do.

Then time passed by, and with it, what?

for love this cannot be,

as such contentment must be more,

than merely love can be.

Where can I search on such a day,

from heat for comfort too,

Such solace would I find within,

your loving arms anew.

THE CURE

I hate the Winter, Summer too,

    and Spring is just like Fall.

And daytime, I can hardly stand

    and night time, not at all.

I do not like the sun that shines,

    and moonlight, does not rate.

I'll go on miserable, cross and mean,

    till love will mellow hate.

I Am Loved

I am loved,
> and in my silent, secret world
> I revel in the wonder of that love.
> The patterns of the world fall into place,
> so easily, so safe, so real.
> I treasure it as no other possession
> in the world.

I am loved
> and he loves me,
> Asks me not, nor questions of my past,
> He wants me, just to see at last
> whenever time may give,
> In him, I live.

I am loved.
> I quietly accept his love,
> Not asking what will be, nor how
> this time will ever last.
> I only know he holds me high in his esteem,
> And I adore this place he gives to me.

I am loved,
> and oh, my stifled heart is free.
> > I am loved.

BREAKUP

That dull hollow feeling deep in the pit of your stomach

    which you can't fill.

The lump in your throat you keep trying to swallow down,

    but it never goes away

The tears, hidden there, just behind that set smile, and the

    warmth of your cheeks from the anger that seems to never fade.

The head held just a little higher than usual,

    although your heart wants to slump.

The lip you bite to hold back the tears.

The sleepless nights, the deep sighs, the endless hours.

    Lying there, listening to the radio, starring at a dark wall.

How well, I know the feeling.

LOVE

What is life but a fleeting, passing, phase,

    so soon rushed by, like restless stormy waves.

How sweet the passionate excitement of memories,

    that play such an important part in holding

    together life.......love.

HE TOUCHES ME

He touches me, not in a physical way,

but with his mind, heart, thought and look.

With words he has to say. And in his eyes, the

mischief lies, when lovingly at play.

His warmth and personality leaves nothing more to read

but fills each sensual surface with its dedicated need.

Although I know, he can't be mine, I treasure moments when

I'm happily in his presence, until we meet again.

He touches me, and gives me breath, so I can live anew.

I surrender to his aura, believing this is true,

Perhaps he can't help seeing the same way that I do,

and yet, perhaps, he lets me touch and hold his feeling too.

I CANNOT SAY

I cannot say, I love you, yet,

       you're someone that I can't forget.

You're charming in a special way

       and thus you cheer my every day.

I'm used to you, like flowers to sun,

       or birds to trees, children to fun.

You're like a part of me somehow,

       a part I cannot disavow

I've come to need you, since we've met,

       but cannot say, I love you…..

         ……….yet!

FOR LOVING ME

You gave me something warm and tender

  to recall, like a lovely song.

Something to cheer me, when I am all alone

  to remember, when you are gone.

Memories are all that remain, but oh,

  what wonderful memories they are.

Each kiss, each caress, so gentle,

  so wonderful, so sweet.

For a while, I was loved, wanted and needed.

  All this you gave to me, without guile or thought.

For this, I thank you, for

  Every lovely dream and memory.

For loving me.

THANKSGIVING

I've never known war. I've never seen hunger and pestilence. I've never known the anguish of family or friend dying in the service. I've never shed tears of fear. I live and work in a large city. My job at times, bores me, and I dream of doing something to give my day some excitement. I ride home secure in the knowledge that I'll get there. My home is safe and warm. There, a hot meal awaits me, and athough I may refuse a second helping of potato, I will accept another chop.

I love to garden and spend many enjoyable hours in my back yard trying to grow radishes, tomatoes and cukes. Not because I cannot buy them, but because of the fun and novelty of growing my own. I sleep in a soft clean bed under my electric blanket. Summer weekends I enjoy a game of golf and look forward to stopping, once in a while for a drink and lunch with a friend.

I grumble about little things, a late bus, being overweight, hard butter, only chocolate ice cream, or having to spend an evening alone to watch TV.

I am not unlike many Americans....who take our green lawns and shade trees for granted. expecting things to be better for us. Feeling that it is absolutely a must that the store shelves be filled to capacity, so we can buy our fill.

Complaining at not having our favorite band at the corner delicatessen. Our morning eggs must be strictly fresh, and so must the bread, Oh, and just the right temperature to the milk I our cereal, and please don't make the coffee too strong!

We are constantly accepting and expecting more. We are God Blessed as a proud people...who stand tall in our own estimation. Too often we forget to appreciate. Too often we fail to kneel, to pray and offer a Thanks-giving.

ODE TO A CLOCK

Ever forward, hour by hour, except for once a year,
When turned one hour backward, but oh, you need not fear,
For once the summers over, you forward march anew.
With spring we gain that hour back, for there's so much to do.
Square or round or oval, on wrists or round the neck,
Whatever shape we read you, time, we're always there to check.
On buildings, stores in various forms, a shelf, a wall, a screen,
Somewhere, somehow no time is lost, as clocks are easily seen.
Yet only when the buzzer sounds to wake us in the morn,
So some clocks garner beatings, yes, bad language, even scorn.
If clocks are wrong, what good ae they? Why are they even kept?
It isn't easy to explain just why you've overslept.
Yet clocks are standard furniture, a part of every life
Tick tocking ever onward, oblivious of strife.
Except for when the power is gone or batteries run dry.
You, clock, just stand, in patience, wait, without a single sigh.
Till someone comes with batteries or key for just a wind,
To give you energy again, when seconds lost, you find.
So clock keep ticking on and on, I know you always will
Till we no longer need you, only then will time stand still

An Interlude

An interlude as Webster states, is

    "an intervening or interruptive space"

Usually where something nice takes place.

    As was this interlude with you.

In your pleasant ways, and in all you do.

    And I needn't mention, you make the nicest view.

So as you make your exodus, I hope you can look back on us.

    Recall in memories numerous,

        this pleasant interlude, a plus.

MMA - FIFTY YEARS LATER

Fifty?   Has it been that long
since I was young and swift and strong?
When in my soul there burned a song
of wonders yet to see.

When did they go so swiftly by?
I can't recall although I try
to see why years just seem to fly
and have forgotten me.

Perhaps the answer lies head.
I still have miles and miles to tread,
although my steps, now feel like lead.
I'm weary as can be.

Between the floor boards, like some sand
some grains slip through, only to land
on slippery water in God's hand.
Is this, then, what I be?

I now this now, I was a fool.
I didn't know I'm just a tool
with which God carves his every rule.
I'm happy to be me.

Although I'm nothing, no one cares,
except, perhaps the Lord upstairs
and of his plans, I'm unawares
just when he'll set me free.

Perhaps in fifty years from now,

someone will read me, and somehow
the poet within will take a bow
as my life was to be.

I'm sure if I would take a poll,
not one of you would change your role.
You've lived your life in your control.
on this you will agree.

So to the fifty still in view,
let's hope there will remain a few
Who'll read this verse, aloud, anew......and then remember me.

MISS YOU

Miss you? Yes my love. Like raindrops miss the clouds above.

Miss you? You know I do like flowers miss the morning dew.

Like springtime longs for April rain, I long to see you once again.

Miss you? Don't you know? Doesn't my heart tell you so?

Now the question, I'll ask you. Tell me, do you miss me too.

FROSTY NIGHT

One frosty mid-December night, the first time that we met,
his eyes sought mine and lingered there, till now, I can't forget.

Throughout that evening, glancing round, one sight I'd always see.
That tender look, in blue, grey eyes, and always fixed on me.

We kissed that night, but only once, a greeting lost in jest,
which lingered in my memory and offered me no rest.

I never saw him after that, but wrote him every day.
And he would answer with sweet words, and songs, for me, he'd play.

That's long ago, yet time stands still on such a frosty night,
Now listening to a radio brings all that time in sight.

Though music soothes a lonely heart, I wonder what would be,
If suddenly we'd meet again, would he remember me?

Only This I Know is Mine

The hours when you are with me,

    to brighten up my day.

The music that is in your voice,

    the tender things you say.

Those happy moments, I'm with you

    just knowing that you care.

Those dreams, so near reality,

    and ours, if we just dare.

The little thoughts you share with me,

    the stories that you tell.

The laughs we have, the silly things,

    which I enjoy so well.

And only this I know is mine,

    this warms my very heart.

It's hard for me to leave you

    for a while to be apart.

LOST LOVE

As each day goes by, and nights slip quickly on,

I feel, again, so hopelessly, how very much is gone.

To know, I once, for just a while,

possessed your love and faith.

Then lost it, oh so rapidly, left hopelessly to wait.

I know each moment slipping by

Means so much more time gone.

So till we, once more, meet again,

we'll know it's all been wrong.

It cannot be that we were meant,

to always be apart, because I feel

that I belong to you, here in my heart.

Perhaps conceit, or something more

Makes me feel you love me too,

But whether this is true or not,

I know that I, oh yes, I do love you.

THROUGH THE DAY

A sunbeam stretched its golden hand across my pillow case.

To try to warm my lonely heart, and cheer my smile less face.

I lay there, thinking of your voice, so warm so deep, so true.

It only made me sadder dear, to want to think of you.

The sun tried once again to cheer, and filled the room with light.

And heartsick, though I felt within, the sunlight made me bright.

I moved to rise and shake my blues, and soon was up and out.

But through the day, the thoughts of you, just followed me about.

Each time the phone or doorbell rang, my heart was filled with glee,

But running there to answer, found, that it was not for me.

Then when the evening finally came, my quest for you was through,

In moonlit dreams, I'd find your love, till the sun woke me anew.

WORRY AND DUTY

My troubles plague me like a locust lot

set down in a field of green.

My soul and spirit, wail and howl,

only yearning to be clean.

Buffeted left and right, and then

beaten and sore I go.

Struggling ever to one end,

to make my misery whole.

To kill the serpent would be fine,

but ah, it's still my heart.

To kill the serpents playmate, then,

would surely be the part?

My writhing hart in torment lay.

I'm caught and cannot pass.

Protect, I must, though die, I will,

to shield my gentle lass.

WHEN PARTING

What can I do?

I cannot cry, I'm much too bold.

I cannot smile I'm much too cold.

I cannot die, my heart is good.

I cannot frown, I'm made of wood.

Yes, made of wood, and tears and dust.

And I can't cry, but yet, I must.

The question that I've asked before

Gets ever louder, more and more.

Why? Why? Why.   Of course I know.

But, why can't I cry? I miss him so.

STONE OF HEART

Only notes sent in silence on wings of a melody borne.

Only thoughts half remembered, but somehow too quickly shorn.

Because of one small empty promise. A note to toss quickly away,

Words which were best left unspoken, now proving there was nothing to say.

Lonely, this spirit seeks solace, carved in the stone of a heart.

Once when love made my being, now it, but tears me apart.

Long will the memory linger, deep in my mind and my soul.

Would that but once it had blossomed, keeping the memory whole.

I WEPT ALONE

No more, no more love, to hurt me thus,

  I will not let it be.

I've often held it close, and felt

  its wrath consuming me.

I feel so empty, like one who is

  sold in bondage.

Love has laughed, and I having laughed with it

  rejoiced, but when I wept,

I wept alone.

I DREAMED OF YOU

I dreamed of you last night, and life took on a warmer hue.

So all the day seemed brighter, filled with happy things to do.

My attitude was cheerful, I had nice things to say.

When lonely thoughts would venture forth, I'd whisk them right away.

I found contentment in my work, I'd chose not to complain,

and though the day was sunny, I'd have even welcomed rain.

Tomorrow may not go as well, but this day was so right.

And all because I dreamed of you, I dreamed of you, last night.

DUMBSTRUCK

It seems when I am near you

    and you're right there to see.

I cannot speak, or say a word,

    or think quite sensibly.

And after you have gone away,

    It's then, that I recall,

The things I wanted mentioned,

    my thoughts come back, yes, all.

I try to keep them with me,

    till the next time you appear.

But once again, I'm dumbstruck,

    when you approach me, dear.

HOPELESS WANTING

The days go by, the hours fly,
the minutes lost in space.
I know you're being torn from me
I feel so out of place.

I long to touch your handsome face,
to kiss your gentle mouth
Yet, in my hopeless wanting,
must learn to do without.

A senseless child, to reach so far,
and grasp at every moon.
But better than to sit and weep
and fill my heart with gloom.

I'll soon forget, I pray to God,
that time will ease the pain
But in my heart, a picture of you,
ever must remain.

CHANCE MEETING

So near, so near to me, my love,

and yet, you could not speak?

Why the trembling hand, the silent look,

Why the courage, oh, so weak?

The surge of love I feel, it isn't wrong or right.

It's foolish, yes, foolish, it blinds my very sight

Oh love what are you? What evil to possess

And never let me be. Keep him from my sight,

From my heart, or very close to me.

To feel, to touch, to kiss his gentle face.

Or hurt, and try to leave him in disgrace.

To think, that he could be so near,

And never speak a word,

To pass me by, as though we never met,

And he had never heard

TOMMY

When the apples are red upon the tree,
but the air's too warm for Fall,
Then the lonely tears I shed for thee
are the times when I'll recall.
When my heart was heaviest with pain
at the thought of never seeing you again,
then my anger at Gods plan
to take you from this life's span,
and leave me here with tears to cry,
I did not think that you would die.
Though my sorrow will long prevail,
One day I will see you through the veil.
When, at last, you greet me too,
and take me home, away, with you.

My dear brother Tommy died October 6, 2004

FRIDAY FAST

My Priest has said my Friday meal

can now be what I wish.

But walk into a restaurant, and all they

have is fish.

THE WRITER OF MUSIC

Oh to have the magic touch

To take a golden strain,

Which fills the air with music

In memory to remain

The gift to write the music

That someone has displayed,

And place with utmost tenderness

Each word and note relayed.

Ah, magic to posses it

It's such a precious treasure

That I, who cannot read or write

Can honor without measure.

Never Change

For every nice thing you do each day,
        no matter how great or small.
For each happy smile, for little things,
        I am grateful for them all.

I know you find it very hard
        to understand my ways.
I 'll try to rearrange my style,
        and halt my words of praise.

Accept my thoughts, as gracefully,
        as I accept your eyes.
Which speak when they are spoken to,
        Yet carefully shield their prize.

You will not change, and nor will I,
        So what we have to do
Is you remain the way you are
        and I"ll keep loving you.

WANDERING SOUL

I am just a wandering soul,

      afloat on Gods great sea.

Unlike it's stanch and dauntless rock,

      I wander aimlessly.

I do not know for what I search

      For help I'm not alone.

A silent prayer plays on my lips

      directing me toward home.

Would that a kinder breeze prevail

      to guide me on my quest.

To lead me safely, there to rest

      So I no longer roam.

HERE

The things I've learned,

The friends I've earned,

The joys we've shared,

Can't be compared.

UNTITLED

Doubless that I love you,

plain as the pain in my heart,

simple as the fear of losing you.

UNTITLED

Variety is the spice of life.

Of this there is no doubt.

And you're the kind of cinnamon

I cannot do without.

UNTITLED

I regret that I had loved you,

for I broke my only heart.

But I will mend it slowly,

and try to make it smart.

UNTITLED

To be yours forever,

in happiness and sorrow.

To possess your wonderous love,

that is my desire.

UNTITLED

My strongest wish, and greatest desire

is your love, in exchange for mine.

My only joy, and deepest pleasure,

is my lips caressing thine.

UNTITLED

Thine eyes revel, thy hidden smile,

thy lips with sunlight kissed.

I look into thine eyes awhile,

and lips cannot resist.

UNTITLED

He is really a man, who can realize,

and admit, to his own mistakes.

UNTITLED

When people talk about you,

with words that are not true,

Remember, that, they are at fault,

the goodness stays with you.

UNTITLED

Each person, in his own element

can be master or clown.

He that is without character

has not, his place, yet found.

UNTITLED

How alike to Spring,

that fills my heart with

warmth and life, to

dash away the gloom.

UNTITLED

The heart that bleedeth not,

knows no pain, no strife.

The heart that bleedeth not,

does not exist in life.

UNTITLED

If trouble wants to get you down,

and life seems less then funny.

Remember me, 'cause, I love you

then life will be quite sunny.

UNTITLED

In New York City, a stranger, must remain.

MODERN PSYCHOLOGY

Forget the past.................

Don't think about the future..........

Ignore the present!

MY HEART SPEAKS

The gentleman smiles, and his
      eyes speak volumes,
Though he does not say a word.
He laughs, and
in a sudden moment,
all tension is gone. Relaxed,
I move about in a world
      I do not know.
He moves his hand and stirs the
      silent world
to fill it with lingering melody.
I am drawn to him, in spite of my
      ever watchful mind.
Oh, master of my soul,
      be wiser than I.
for I am lost in fantasy,
unwilling to give in to reality
yet, afraid, to remain in tender dreams

FIRST KISS

The smile of ecstasy that plays
upon my lips, when I am all alone.
Is what is left of memories that linger,
of dreams that I have known.
Your tender kiss that bearly touched my lips,
yet meant so much and made me thrill
right to my fingertips.

Hoped for love, such as I had,
yet unexpected, too.
Could only mean, you hoped for me,
and wanted my love, too.
Ah, sweet the kiss, that now remains
within my lonely heart.

How can it be, so real to me, yet
seems forgotten on your part.
My sighing heart, like fire burns,
then silently, the smile of ecstasy returns.

SHARING

Like breakfast on weekends, and work that we do.

Shopping on Broadway, and lunches there too.

Watching TV. whether favorite or not.

Snacks and warm milk, and I almost forgot

      things like.....

Coffee on the porch in the Summer.

Lunch under the apple tree, in the rain.

Both of us in the same corner of a big yard, and

      getting in each others way.

Folding curtains, laughing at something silly, and

      crying over our grief.

I love you very much my darling.

Thank you for sharing your life with me.

      a note to my Mom

My Annie

When God, one day, in warm July placed
  our dear Annie in our life.
It was because he knew from all
  she'd be the one who'd thrive.
The one who could, if she but choose,
  be anything she dare.
And thus he let her be the first,
  because he knew she'd care.
As sister to us all, we loved her as the best,
  respected, held in high esteem
through every kind of test.
She weathered storms, we might have shunned.
  She braved the hardest road.
Then in the end God helped her through
  to carry one last load.
I miss you sister, more than breath.
  You were so close to me.
I hope I proved to be, the kind of sister, I
  should be.
The only thing I now can do,
  write you in poetry.
I love you still, I always will, until my
  grieving heart,
will know throughout eternity,
  we'll never be apart.

GROWING UP

When I was young and frivolous

I thought that men were chivalrous.

Then as the years passed by,

so many caught my eye.

I found that now I'm older,

they really are much bolder.

To Someone Sweet

Take all the nicest adjectives,

and all the sweetst phrases,

There still would be abundant space,

in which to sing you praises.

It's rare to find a lovely flower,

which aura never ends.

I'm happy that, I'm numbered too,

among your many friends.

SLEEPLESS NIGHT

The salt from my tears

has dried on my cheek,

leaving a trail of white.

Evidence that once again,

yes, again,

I have spent a sleepless night.

CHILDREN AT PLAY

Today I heard the angels laugh

a light and lillting sound.

That filled my heart with wonderous joy,

and warmed the world around.

It was the sound of children playing

their voices echoed cheers.

It seemed like I've not heard that sound

In oh so many years.

REPORT FROM FRAN KULIK WHILE WORKING AT WEBR RADIO

When finally, I do arrive, to do my full days calling I plunge right in, to check and right* (*correct) The copy, most appalling. Correct mistakes, and cut 'em down, because most every agency make minutes last much longer, to make a fool of me. I write for certain sponsors, from cars to bakers fair. And what I say about them, is honest, straight and square. I get my copy ready, and then with lovey look.

I hand all this to Shirley E, who says, "Let's check the book." Acknowledgements I answer, to those who want it so.

"Yes Sir, we have received your discs, just thought you'd like to know."

The daily ads, I try so hard, to have them read by folk, And find at times things do backfire, and land like some sad joke. To add to chores I work at, the switchboard for relief And "Listen While" at certain times, a pleasant stint but brief. I must admit, I love my work, and all who work with me. And find the folks most pleasant, agreeable as can be And thus, my talents vary, still my wandering mind will cling, To songs I'd like to publish and also someday, sing.

To My Readers

How can I say it, the word I want

    to one who's seen my soul?

I'm glad to know you read my work,

    and though my mind I still control,

my wandering makes me out....a fool?

    No......rather a dreamer, I would say.

But thanks for seeing what others don't see,

    And hearing what I literately here say.

LOVE'S TWICE BLESSED

Love's twice blessed by those with vision,

    cursed by those of indecisiion.

Now it's glory, but too late,

    one discovers useless hate.

Love is sharing, not pretending,

    there will be a happy ending.

Would that love would not provoke,

    that would be a happy joke.

Love's promiscuous, but alas

    promiscuity has to pass.

Though we strive for love unending,

    It's a road that has a bending.

Love's heartbreaking, without doubt,

    Yet something life can't be without.

ESCAPE

Oh, give me the quiet and peace of the sea,

    and a home by a cliff, which will just shelter me.

But give me no lover, to make nights go fast,

    just good and lost memories, of things in the past.

Then give me, by chance, a glad offer of words,

    or maybe a kiss, by a number of birds.

Or give me a storm on a hot Summer day,

    or a night filled with music, and stars bright with play.

Give me a chance to go back to the past,

    relive once again, when I saw him last.

Then take me, enfold me, and ask once anew.

    Are you sorry that he, loved the sea, more than you.

Who

Who will lull away my fears?

    Bring me, often times, near tears,

        With the music that he plays,

            Or the way he turns a phrase?

Who will wake me in the night?

    With a song that brings delight.

        Filling me with warm desire

            Thrilling me with burning fire?

Who, if not the warmth of you?

    Who, when no one else will do.

        Since that door has finally slammed,

            Leaving me alone, and damned.

THE FIRE IS OUT

I think perhaps the fire is out,

    the ash has all turned gray.

The embers that once flickered life,

    have slowly died away.

The flutter in my heart is stilled,

    the sighs, now sound regret.

The sparkle that once filled my eyes,

    are dim unless their wet.

My dream was not reality,

    when faced with simple lies,

I've nothing left to fool my heart,

    which mourns itself, and cries.

REFLECTION OF MY MOTHER

There are times when you're a mother,

 there are times when you're a friend.

There are times when we're like sisters,

 as the road of life we wend.

Dear, I treasure every moment,

 for your thoughtful, generous ways,

Cause you've taught me countless lessons,

 some with scolding, most with praise.

Till you've made me into something ,

 that is happy, kind and true.

A reflection of my mother,

 I'm so proud to be like you.

WHEN MOM WAS IN THE HOSPITAL

The extra little mothers touch,

that makes a room so bright.

The warmth that makes a house, a home,

and keeps our troubles light.

That something which is missing

only you can fill that place.

The loneliness, the silence, that

your smile will soon erase.

Although it may not seem that much,

we feel so lost and blue.

And want you, soon, back home with us,

for Mom we all love you.

WOULD YOU LOVE ME?

Would you love me if you went away?

    If you left me now, if you didn't stay?

Would you love me I my fire grew cold,

    If I'd spent my youth, if I now was old?

Would you love me, were I deep in debt?

    If I get so now, will you soon forget?

Would you love me, if I weren't spring to

    your autumn life, would that be the thing?

Could you see me then, would I be a bore?

Would you love me, I have doubts, somehow,

    Would you love me? Do you love me now?

WAKENING

My warm bed beckons, and I go to sleep, to fall into

  beautiful dreams of you,

wherein you hold me close, and kiss away my fears.

My troubles disappear like dew upon the morning rose.

My heart is filled with the wonder of you,

  and oh, my love it shows.

On awakening, my happiness bubbles over

  to fill my heart with cheer, and color my cheek,

where you have kissed me, when you held me near.

You brought me so much joy in dreams,

  yet know me not, awake, it seems.

LOVE IS

Love is mental and physical attraction,

in emotional insecurity.

TOURS

We meet as strangers, but day by day,

Our awkward feelings just fade away.

Through conversation, sights and sounds,

We push our shyness, out of bounds.

Then as our journey quickly ends,

We come away with new found friends.

WITH EVERY BREATH

With every breath, you speak his name, with ever thought you smile.

With every heartbeat it's the same, he's with you all the while.

With evey tick of time that's past, you wonder what is real.

How long can all this magic last, how much time can we steal?

When weakened by a tender look, when my arms cry for you.

What will we do to break this web, how can we say it's through?

To consumate in final trial, thus to begin, or end.

With loving kisses, we might last, or cursed, understand.

For this we tremble on the brink, we're both afraid to cross,

And only time will tell, if this, will be our gain, or loss.

We, You and I

This one thing I know to be
        your heart is young as mine.
In this our love is like to those
        that live on sands of time.

We linger when we ought to go.
        We laugh, while others weep.
We think until were tired and weak,
        and yet we cannot sleep.

This one thing I know is sad,
        we're lost before we start.
Forever you are bound onto,
        an ever faithful heart.

So I must hold my head erect,
        to stifle sob and sigh.
But this one thing I know to be
        We love, we, you and I.

MISTAKE

You'd think by now, I'd know the route,
>   my sorrow now is aboslute.
You'd think I'd learned, I thought I had,
>   but once again, I fell, and bad.
With open eyes I stormed right in,
>   to dangers where I once had been.
In writhing agony am I,
>   surrounded by a loveless cry,
and vow again though fool I be.
>   This cannot happen, not to me!
I've learned my lesson, once or twice,
>   yet cannot take my own advice.
May heaven help this hopeless lass,
>   and help this agony to pass.
For once again I've lost my heart.
>   to prove I'm really not too smart.
For love, though beautiful and free,
>   has shown, again, it's not for me.

ANOTHER NOTE FROM THE MISTY LADY

Yes, stay I will, I can't resist, the fate of one who has been kissed,
By lips so warm, though garlic scented.   For lingering strength
No doubt intended.
Oh, I'll hold fast and do my bit, to win your heart, I'll never quit.
I've stormed, too often wilder seas, to lose them all to jealousies.
And jealous though indeed I be, I can't deny thy loving plea
For every song, for me, you play, to bid the Misty lady stay.
But mark ye well, don't think me cute, t'was thee who once
Called me astute.
Which means I know before I'm told and can't be fooled by
Wiles of old.
Confused? At best, I must admit, I love to keep you thus, a bit.
But you are sharp, and know me well, though at a distance.
What the .ell.
I'm speaking of your five, or six, say, misty ladies just don't mix.
There's only one, on true and tough, this one alone should
Prove enough.
Which other lover sends you tea, or lifts your spirits joyfully?
And if, at time, I seem quit terse, who else, but I,
Writes you I verse?
So tease me not too badly so, I'll have to find elsewhere to go.
I love you true, but what the heck, I have to switch to Georgie Beck.

LOVE

What is life but a fleeting, passing, phase?

So soon rushed by like restless stormy waves.

How sweet the passionate excitement of memories,

that play such an important part in holding

together life…..love.

WORDS UNSPOKEN

Your words bespeak a willing heart,

  but words, alone, are cold.

You cannot kiss an alphabet

  for what is there to hold.

I crave the strength of two strong arms,

  and lips with sweet caress.

That crush me to submission,

  with utmost tenderness.

Ah, dreams are dust, in which I see,

  a loneliness for me.

Then words unspoken, dreams, but mist,

  will fail dramatically.

THE LITTLE BUD BLOOMS

The little bud blooms, a wonderous flower

  for all the world to see.

It's perfume to enjoy, so sweet,

  so filled with ecstasy.

And I recall, I once was there,

  when, yet, this bloom was seed.

I saw, in time, this come to pass

  my flower, was not a weed.

Ah, blossemed voice thy bloom is rare,

  such sweet and vintage years

have now my soul enchanted

  and fills me now with tears.

Would that these lips could render thus

  a sonnet mine by birth.

What comfort to my aching heart,

  what joy to all the earth.

SHORT EXCEPTS

Love, a sudden burst of unprotected emotion
moved along by the softness of song,
the magic of moonlight, or other dreamy thought.

THE GAME IS WON

Pride takes still another fall.

    Each blow only adding to my wealth

of hard earned facts.

    For now, I take life in my stride,

I know how it works.

    Hunger does not teach, but fracture pride,

and leaves you, worthless, mortified.

UNKNOWN

And thus my heart has died, in this brief encounter

    standing face to face with a ghost.

The years that have past, seem such illusions.

    The phanton I have dreamed of, which I try to see

in every person, is a sham. He never existed,

    only, perhaps in my own imaginative mind.

But I loved him, real or no, I loved him

    and the glow of it still remains.

From his voice as he sang, to the frown

    that he wore when we parted.

He hurled me from his life and I, like a boulder

    lay atrophying in my anquish. Unable to,

    unwanting any other.

And if there should be one that breaks through he

    lasts but for a while till I find him not worthy to be

    classed in the same realm of men as he.

GOODBYE

I think perhaps the fire is out,

    the ash has all turned gray.

The embers that once flickered life,

    have slowly died away.

The flutter in my heart is stilled,

    the sighs now sound regret.

The sparkle that once filled my eyes,

    are dim unless their wet.

The dream was not reality,

    when faced with simple lies.

I've nothing left to fool my heart

    which mourns itself and cries.

COLD OR FLU?

You attack my eyes
      my throat, my ears, my nose
      keeps running like my tears.
I cough, I wheeze, I try to sleep
      but end up in a troubled heap,

A potty call each hour or two
      just robs me of my rest.
I'll be so dragged out in the morn,
      I'll never do my best.

Within a week I'll still be sore
      my aches will not subside.
And how I feel, and how I look
      is something I can't hide.

There's only one advantage,
      I've noticed that of late
In spite of all this misery,
      I've also lost some weight.

A LITTLE POEM

Because it's such a lovely day,

because I'm feeling good.

I thought I'd write a poem for you,

and decided that I would.

And so these little words enclosed,

as here I've indicated,

Are just for you, for you alone,

and to you dedicated.

GLAD I'M ME

I know I'm nothing special,

    and few will know my name.

But I know that God made me,

    so I have little shame.

For he has made a plan for me,

    as what I can or cannot be.

Successful to a small degree,

    at least, I'm glad I'm me.

Hope You Remember

The least you could do, since you're going away,

    is let me see more of you, now, every day.

Then I can store up every memory of you

    the way that you smile and the things that you do.

So when we're apart, I won't pine, no, or cry

    for, I'll miss you so, when you bid me goodbye.

And I hope you'll remember, as long as I do,

    The fact that I loved you, so much, for it's true.

No Tears

No tears, my grief lies deeper than shining tears,
      I've known him for so many years
I've lived his life, as yet my own,
      No tears, although I am alone.
No tears, though kindly words are good to hear,
      and friendly hugs, which try to cheer.
These are the grown, of seeds he's sown.
      and yet, he too, was all alone.
Who will remember him, but I?
      Who at his grave, will often cry?
There's no one, now to carry on.
      When once, I too, will then, be gone.
No one to tend, to place a flower,
      or stand and pray for half an hour.
I come to visit, no one sees,
      and only God can hear my pleas.
No tears can now erase my woe,
      but, I have nowhere else to go.
I'll dry my eyes, and go my way,
      to once again return one day.

APOLOGIES

I'd love to come to your soiree'

      to laugh and chat and play,

To be with folks I love to see,

      for more than half a day.

But alas, my day is booked from

      early morn till eve.

And if I came, for just a while,

      too soon, I'd have to leave.

No Regrets

As bargain bought, he cast his lot

　　and charmed me, more than twice.

Then tossed me like a broken toy,

　　into his world of ice.

Now don't you preach, with useless words,

　　what was to be, has been.

If he has speared me with his wrath,

　　I've left my mark on him.

MORE NOTES FROM THE MISTY LADY

Dear BK

Two weeks, I woke with anger. My morning was not right.

I grumped at everyone all day, which stretched into the night.

I went to see a doctor, who told me all was well.

Yet I could not dispel the gloom, that in my heart would swell.

Then one AM, I turned the dial, tilll your voice filled the room.

then all the cheer was back, to warm and paint my cheeks with bloom.

You've woke me, far too long a time, for me to change my way.

and though you've left the area, on my dial, you have to stay.

As I do not read the radio column, I didn't know about your move,

and am at a loss as to where you went. I hope it's a happy move for

you. Good luck and good health from the Misty Lady

MAY YOUR LIFE BE

May your life be

Like the music you play.

Full of yesterday's pleasant memories,

Yet ready for the promise of tomorrow.

SHORT THOUGHTS

Don't think about the future,

And just ignore the present,

Keep your head in the sand.

Then wonder why life is so hard.

A GOOD MORNING?

Why is it that few minutes in the morn

when I should be astir?

Is just the time I get the languid pleasurable sleep

that I longed for through the night.

THE DEMISE OF MUSIC

Where have the old songs gone?
　　　The ones that sung of sweet delight
Which hummed on endless through the night.
　　　That made you want to dance or sing,
Or send your heart out on the wing.
　　　Which entertained melodiously
or made us laugh in simple glee.
　　　No hard core lessons to implore,
Or heartless visions to restore.
　　　just music, pure and simple yet,
something that one would not forget.
　　　Those songs that we still sing today
which were big hits of yesterday,
　　　might now again be nicely stored,
If folks were not so awfully bored
　　　with turning dials to hear a tune
that doesn't blow one's mind with gloom,
　　　or noise that's in the guise of song.
Ah yes, where has our music gone?

CONSOLATION

I'd like to sit and weep with you,
      to share your hurt and pain.
As friend in need, who has to cry,
      without the fear of shame.
To linger, for a little while
      on all the joys, the fun,
To keep a hold on feelings
      where somehow, you want to run.
To hear you reprimand yourself
      for patience on your part
To sew together all the tears.
      within your broken heart.
To say, things will be better now,
      the cobwebs are swept clean,
To tell you to refresh your soul,
      and start a brand new dream
But words are simply words, that's all,
      no consolation there,
But merely blotters for your tears
      when no one seems to care.
Oh, let me say I understand
      in some small way I do.
I'm really sad, you're sorely hurt,
      I sympathize with you.

This was written as an annivesary gift for my Aunt Mary (Kulik) Krajcer. Unfortunately, I never dated it.

CHILDHOOD MEMORIES

Can it be all that long ago with crates, a store we'd fix, and play with dry corn and old felt hats, and funny, glass like sticks.
When Babka's house was one warm place where we enjoyed each day, and looked, so forward to return, when 'er we went away.
Where our Aunt Mary washed our hair, in one, round enormous tub, and then our knees and knuckles too, she'd dearly soak and scrub.
At times we'd play some games with her Fan, Tan, oh, that was fun. Of course she played, not well at all, somehow, we, always won.
And puzzles had a way of being easier to fill, when Marys hand would move with ours to fill a muraled still.
These memories come winging back, as I take pen in hand. Warm,
cheerful, happy days of yore, I know were truly grand.
The kitchen door, the rack of cloths, that hung along the wall, and next to it, a rocker, with a back that seemed sooo tall.

(The small hall into the kitchen, where the cat would let himself in by putting his paw into a small hole on the bottem edge and pulling the door open. What was his name? I think it was Whitey.)

"Smechnieck" (a medicine) that smelled like birch beer, which Babka drank at times, for her aches and pains. A sink in the kitchen which was dark blue. During a thunderstorm we were always warned not to go near it, because of lightning strikes.

Button mushrooms frying on the top metal plate on the stove.
A tasty thing to do.

(Sandwichs made with mustard and sugar, bananas, or canned milk sprinkled with sugar then toasted.)

The grand old stove with roaster of meat, that sat a way, way back.

God's Pencil

You could nibble any time, with help from a grownup. There never was a lack.
And, Oh, those chocolate baskets, with handles you could eat at Easter time.
      What candy man concocted such a special treat.
The time when Smokes creek flooded and filled the whole first floor of the
house, and we all slept upstairs, for a night of two or maybe more, on big
old feather beds we dragged from out of their cozy room, with reassurances
      to us,the water would leave soon.
The sounds of laundry washing, and ticking of the clock, the rumbling of the
      railroad train, behind the house, or down the block.

Father Justins radio hour, or nightime baseball game. Someone was always
      listening for the times were calm and tame.
      The front hall, that seemed to be a place you couldn't go. The couch that
stretched into a bed. I loved when lights were low.
A white marble dresser, with a mirror, tall and wide. When Uncle Stash would
      chase me, the small table, where I'd hide.

(The red raspberries on the fence in the back yard, next to the old garage.)
The chickens underneath the house, or hen coop in the yard, where we would
      look for fresh laid eggs, the kind that weren't hard.
The barrel full of rainwater, the marvelous back yard swing, where i would
      entertain myself to sit and softly sing.
The stripped down car where we would play, all seems like a mirage, and all
      the treasures you could find, within the old garage.

On rainy days , old flower sacks, we wore like hooded elves, to wade along
      the gutter in the street, not by ourselves.

(The trips to the plasoo (woods).   the baseball games behind the trestle)

And piling pennies into rolls, was just within our reach, or riding on a carousel,
way down at Woodlawn beach.
We rubbed small sand bricks into sand, and walked between the track, and
gazed into the colored glass, or lanterns painted black.
And I remember carbon stone, that shone with color bright, when you would
      hold it in your hand, reflecting warm sunlight.

Monoply was newer then. How often you would see, the gang playing in
front of
       Babka's house, beneath that hugh old tree.

(The fat green caterpillers we tried to kill with vinegar and salt)

The old man, Mr. Sherman, who tried,in vain, to feed me, at your Wedding
       reception   I was a little girl. The way we, my sister and I, cried
       when you were leaving for your honeymoon.

These memories are all too clear. Has time gone by that slow? Or is it that
       they're still as dear, as they were long ago?
Whatever's true, I'm glad that I could easily remember, to put these thoughts
       in verse for you, this fourteenth of September.
So in the future years you'll see the new blend with the old, and memories are
       things that keep us warm, when life seems growing cold.

WHAT IS A MOM?

Mom, is a soothing hand on a child's fevered brow

    A kind word, when everything goes wrong.

The lady, who stays up till after you've come home

    late in the A.M.

Knowing you are troubled before you tell her.

    Having a surprisingly correct answer.

Being understanding, when you least expect it.

    Setting the table for breakfast the night before,

even if she doesn't get up to make it.

    Wanting the best for you, instead of for herself.

Forgiving with a hug and loving you always.

    That is a Mom.

SIGN

Those things that used to please you are no more.

Living is mundane, laughter is for fools.

And picking at the ugly things in life is the thought of the day.

The sunlight no longer delights and rising in the morning

is only a sign that there is a day before you, to work.

It is, as if, the soul is longing to go home to a more peaceful place.

It is a sign that you no longer care for him.

MEMORY OF YOU

My time with you, so warm, so brief,
      and stolen like a lowly thief,
Are treasures in my memory,
      these precious moments spent with thee.

Though fate decrees all things must change,
      I would not have it rearrange
my life, to be a different hue,
      it's all, a wondrous thing with you.

This tender game will not desist,
      I revel in each gentle kiss.
And beg no promise, nor remorse,
      but wend my way, where leads your course.

Then, as I wander on my way,
      If, but to hold your hand each day,
I'll garner to my heart what's due,
      a happy memory of you.

WOULD THAT SUCCESS COULD SMILE

Would that success could smile on me,

      as it has done on you.

I'd surely wear a happy face, and

      and never more be blue.

Would that I had you Midas touch,

      that turns the world to gold.

What dreams would this fulfill for me,

      what longings, yet untold?

Would that I had your outlook,

      life, so dauntlessly you face.

My worried days would just be one,

      and doubt, I could erase.

Would that the future treats you kind,

      and with you all the while,

stays happiness and, yes, success

      continue long to smile.

WIND

Wind wakes me from my sleep

And shouts in whispered words

That I do not understand.

And thus it goes throughout the night,

Waking and sleeping, restlessly,

Until the morning arrives.

LONELY MEMORIES

How silent is the world tonight

    no breath of air, no bird in flight.

The heavy air weighs down on me

    like grief that keeps me company.

Though sadly standing near her grave,

    no solace does my heart embrace.

What merit, then to stand and sob?

    to feel alone, and cry to God.

She's gone and I, alone must cry

    too soon, I had to say goodbye.

Somehow she seems more near to me

    here in the quiet cemetery.

Her body, is no longer here, her voice

    will someday disappear.

But in my heart I'll cherish these

    most poignant, lonely memories

I WISH I HAD A SON

I wish I had a son, a brand new baby boy

Who'd fill his fathers life with dreams

And mine with endless joy.

I wish I had a girl, all pink and soft to hold.

To warm my lonely everyday,

And make my life less cold.

I wish I had a child, a child to call my own.

To bundle very carefully

and take into my home.

MAGIC TOUCH

Oh to have the magic touch

    to take a golden strain,

which fills the air with music

    in memory to remain.

To write it down on paper

    a tune to sing or play.

How lucky to be able to

    and do it every day.

The gift to hear the music,

    that someone else has played.

And place with utmost tenderness

    each word and note relayed.

Ah, magic to possess it,

    this, such a precious gift.

For me, who cannot read or write,

    what treasure would I give?

VALENTINE SONG

This odd valentine greeting is sent from the heart

'Twas written a long time ago.

When my way of expressing the way that I felt,

With no way of letting you know.

But now, I must send it, for you did inspire

my soul to such heights it was lent,

That thus is the music, the lyrics, I wrote

The song that through my heart was sent.

SOLITUDE

It is not that my lot is low,
      that bids this silent tear to flow.
It is not my grief that hides my moan,
      it is that I am all alone.
In woods and glens I love to roam.
      when the tired hedger hies him home.
Or by a woodland pool to rest,
      when pale the star looks on its breast.
Yet when the silent evening sighs,
      with hollowed airs and symphonies,
My spirit takes another tone,
      and sighs that it is all alone.
The autumn leaf is sear and dead,
      it floats upon the waters bed.
I would not be a leaf to die
      without recording sorrows sigh.
The woods and winds, with sudden wail
      tell all the same unvaried tale.
I've none to smile when I am free,
      and when I sigh, I sigh with me.
Yet in my dreams I form a view,
      that thinks on me, and loves me too.
I start, and when the visions gone
      I weep that I am all alone.

WHAT'S GONE?

Where flames lept bright, an embered ash remains,

and former lovers now revert to games.

Those lips no longer speak of love,

and hands that once clung tight, remain in glove.

A moment treasured now, is lost to time,

but I, a hungry dreamer cling to mine.

A look avoided, for fear that eyes reveal,

the smothered emptyness they feel.

What's gone, that I should feel this way?

The magic which was there has gone away.

We now, no longer feel that we are one,

The time has fled with so much left undone.

WINTER'S DISPLAY

The mass of earth, once colored green, has turned into a place

where no such beauty has been seen, except Gods holy space.

The glow of diamonds glitter, on roof tops bright with snow,

to vanish in the month of May, in rivulets will flow.

The winds have turned the ponds to ice, now shining massive clear,

where skate blades soon will whiz across, and laughter we will hear.

Though not a sign of life prevail, the pine in comfort slept,

In snows that hold a simple trail where mouse or deer have crept.

The stars are splashed upon a canvas, blue, mixed in with clouds of grey.

The scene of beauty sketched by who?

By God, in this, his own Winter Display.

I Can't

Would that I could

    in eloquent phrase,

Speak what my heart feels is true.

But love is a thing

    only poets can sing,

In verses both lovely and blue.

You know how I feel,

    and my feeling is real.

But to say it aloud

    no, I shan't.

Not that I don't,

    not that I won't,

but simply because dear,

    I can't.

TIME WITHOUT YOU

It seems a week, stretched into months,

    And months into a year.

And years into a century,

    When you're not close, my dear.

A minute is, now an hour,

    And hour, is now a day.

And days fly by, yet, drag so long,

    While you are far away.

It seems, my heart has lived complete

    It's dream of us, till now,

The understanding, that, I'm lost

    Without you near, somehow.

ANOTHER THANK YOU NOTE

I thank you once and twice and thrice

and have to say "That was awfully nice."

The show was great, the audience cheered,

and gee, I actually met the "beard".

(I have no idea who that was)

THE SIGH

He said not a word, and she too, spoke no more.

So, thus the gap between then grew, bigger than before.

And life was one sad moment, followed by another.

And yet, they knew within their hearts, that they still loved each other.

But some small hurt had happend, that neither, now remember.

until the silence reigned, till love, was just a little ember.

Then one day she so deeply sighed, and he so quickly turned,

That in that sudden moment, the ember brightly burned.

Then love was stronger than before and bound them tighter still.

So now and then, each time she sighs, she smiles, and always will.

PARDON ME LIFE

Pardon me life, but I've allowed myself

    the luxury of falling in love.

Tenderly and completely, without too much

    excitement or problem.

As easily as I breathe, or feel. The warmth of it

    fills me with renewed energy and youth.

I am free to love and live with a smiling face

    and a lighter happier step.

TREASURE

Were it upon my lips to say,
    the times I've thought of you.
In countless numbers day be day
    when I'm alone and blue.

I've treasured moments when we've laughed,
    and times when love was play.
I've held you close in memories,
    refreshed with what you say.

At moments when I can't go on,
    when sorrow fills my night.
One thought of you, one fleeting thought,
    and there is joy and light.

You've filled my life with much delight.
    I want to tell you so.
I treasure every thought of you
    and just want you to know.

VACATIONS

When on vacation in a sunny clime,

remember to keep this rule.

When indoors, keep your inside warm,

When outside, play it cool.

JUST WAITING

Unknown to those around me, here, my head

is well aware, of an emply, lonely feeling,

just because you are not there.

I feel your thoughts are with me, still it's

strange how much I yearn,

and with warm anticipation,

anxiously wait for your return.

CLING TO LIFE

Ah, sleep, sleep, thy avenging angel, wakefulness

robs me of my need.

The familiar torment steals within my heart,

and I am but a frail receptacle

no longer able to survive.

Then a stronger enemy, jealousy consumes me

and burns me, again to cinder of stone.

Better I were dead, then left alone,

So I must cling to life, or flee.

FAREWELL BELOVED

Farewell beloved, I shall not weep

      for comfort comes on soft, swift feet

      to chase away the blues from my poor heart.

Farewell beloved, I shall not cry

      for kisses wipe my tear stained eye,

      and dry the tears before they even start.

Farewell my dream, my empty dream

      I could have loved you so.

Goodbye my heart, my darling heart,

      too bad you did not know

Farewell beloved, I shall not weep

      for comfort comes on soft, swift feet

      to quench the lonliness that's left by you

      and try to fill the love that once I knew.

BROKEN PROMISE

I've thrown in the towel,
I've waved the white flag
I've yelled and yelled "uncle"
Till I almost could gag.
I've given you up for the 85th time,
It doesn't make sense that
I wish you were mine.
Yet, I find I'm relenting
I'm no longer mad.
I don't think you are awful,
Or awfully bad.
Although you ignore me,
you are not in the way,
at least I'm creating a new
verse every day.
So I'll take back my towel and white
flag for a truce
Sigh one more deep sigh and
Say "Hell what's the use!"
Tomorrow I'll love him. Like I have once before.
Till the next broken promise
lays me flat on the floor.

DEAR FRIEND

Some day, when I am older, and sense makes me wise,

I'll look back on these memories with tears in my eyes.

Then perhaps I'll regret all the lonely days wasted,

or revel in thoughts of some sweet moments tasted.

But whichever will be, you're a part of my heart.

From the moment we met, till death tears us apart.

But for what earthly reason were you placed in my life.

I shall ever be curious, I can't be your wife or sister,

or lover, so I have to contend

with being just me, a sincerely ' dear friend.'

YOU RETURN

When I am nestled in your arms,

    must time go by so fast?

Or when your lips are pressed to mine,

    can't magic moments last?

I treasure every lovely hour,

    when I am close to you.

And wait impatient as a flower,

    that longs for morning dew.

I rush into your warm embrace

    your arms around me tight.

And am content to stay right there,

    throughout my day and night.

SHORT THOUGHTS

The brushing of two pair of lips.

The love potion that promises so much,

and guarantees so little.

SHORT THOUGHTS

Many a promise made in the dead of night,

hold a different meaning in the morning light.

SHORT THOUGHTS

To be given dreams, that two can share,

is a prayer.

SHORT THOUGHTS

Be my eyes, my life, my soul.

Be the breath I breathe, and the thoughts I think.

Be my guide, my protector, my heart and mind.

For I love blindly, and lean upon you.

SHORT THOUGHTS

Be thou mine, forever be, loving me eternally,

Till the day no longer brings,

promises of brighter things.

SHORT THOUGHTS

If all the world were wont to flower,

Yet we sat, idly, hour by hour.

Who then would earn our daily dower?

SHORT THOUGHTS

If I tell you, go, is it not better to know love

    as a beauteous thing, not as an arduous passion,

to be remembered in love, than forgotten in regret?

SHORT THOUGHTS

Someome, somewhere, dreams of your smile,

and while thinking of you, thinks that life is worthwhile.

So whenever you're lonely, remember it's true,

someone, somewhere is thinking of you.

SHORT THOUGHTS

Memories too often fade,

of things we like to treasure.

So write them down, and on return,

recall each day with pleasure.

BEWILDERED

You're sure of me, I see it now,
    that smugness in your look.
Your certain of my every step.
    my goose is yours to cook
I beg of you, don't trample me,
    don't wring me dry, don't maim.
I'll be your willing victim though,
    I can't enjoy the pain.
I hate this game you play with me,
    I cringe each time you laugh.
I don't now if your with me or
    have I been torn in half.
Perhaps I've known too much deceit
    to tell what I should do,
I wish that you would take the time,
    to see what I go through.
Then you could be much kinder
    and every now and then
You'd hug me close, to let me know
    you love me as a friend.

THOUGHTS OF YOU

Beyond my hope, within my heart
the memory of you is dear
I find my mind is still with you,
when you're no longer here.

A step behind me, and I smile,
your voice still makes me thrill.
How often with your single look,
my head begins to whirl.

What is this charm you hold for me?
What sheer delight to know,
that when the day has slipped on by,
my thoughts of you will grow.

Then through the night
I'll dream of you and hope a new found day.
Will send me where I'll be with you,
to hear the words you say.

ERIE COUNTY FAIR

Every year when I was there

 I so enjoyed the yearly fair.

I wandered through the thronging mass,

so crowded yet you let them pass.

And as the years went by I knew,

I had to win a prize or two.

So I grew flowers, or baked a pie,

I'd win a ribbon, or at least I'd try.

I do have blue, which passed the test

But never got the white for best.

Now, years have taken toll on me

I'm not as spry as I once could be.

So now I go to buy my treats

I'm still so very fond of sweets.

I sit and simply watch the folks

All varied sizes, different strokes.

Enjoying simply being there

The yearly Erie County Fair.

WHY I LOVE MUSIC

I love it for the happy memories,
      that pass over a wrinkled brow,.
Of silent revories of romance once held
      so near and now so far away.
Of those I loved and so silently accept
      their fate.
They are happy, they do not regret, I
      made them wait.
I love it for the words of wisdom
      it has sung into my ears,
Yet,warnings not to lose my heart,
      fell not until the tears.
The glad, the light, the troubled heart,
      has often been released
From many sore and troubled times
      for only a moment grasped,
Till the music ends, and the dreams are
      passed.

TODAY I NEED

A friend

    to reassure me.

    to comfort me.

    to cheer me.

    to love me.

And still, within me,

    I have that friend who shares

    my lonliness,

    my empty dreams, and

    my unrequited love.

So why can't I... comfort.....

    me.

MELODY OF CHIMES

I know truly, Jesus loves me
      'cause he tells me so.
With each ray of golden sunshine,
      with the flowers that grow.
When the clouds bring Summer showers,
      even when there's snow
I know Jesus walks beside me
      ever present, ever watchful, this I truly know.
When my heart feels full of sadness,
      though I sometimes cry.
I feel Jesus holds me closely,
      wipes my tear stained eye.
With the song that Jesus sends me,
      through my wind blown chimes.
I know he is always with me,
      even in hard times.
So the answer that I'm seeking
      can't be far away.
I know Jesus always loves me
      each and every day.

SPRING THOUGHTS

You can't be sad on a day like this,

    the sun fillls the earth witht its radiance.

The sky is an endless blue,

    The bushes and trees are bursting with bloom.

Everywhere the world has come alive.

    In silence and beauty. God has, once again,

        given people a reason for living.

WITH WORDLESS LOOK

Would that my heart, so fat with tears

      could burst its dikes and woefully cry,

      releasing me from torment and grief.

Would that I, like clouds above when

      overwhelmed, shed their tears.

Which lad has made me bleed so blue?

Yet I, the lass, in sadness, press a

      tearless eye, in sight of thee,

When in a foreign place I saw the one of which

      my heart has dearly sought, but not alone.

Which thereby placed me in this woe.

Would that I could but hide my heart,

      so that you somehow know, with wordless look

      to say how very much, I love you so.

VISION

There is no longer flesh upon thy lovely cheek

For death ravashes within your grave do seek.

The golden hair may then remain, and yet,

How can I see thee only after death?

What final vision was that which I had viewed,

You waved a greeting not to be distraught.

to wipe away the anquish that death brought.

Did I indeed see hope in heaven's view?

I saw you as the one I loved and knew.

So full of life and happily moving on.

To find your way to God who, now you found.

MONDAY THRU FRIDAY

Today is Monday. It's blue and damp....
        I wish I had a postage stamp.
        I try to work, but find I can't.
        Thank goodness Tuesday's near.
Today is Tuesday, sunny and bright.
        I didn't sleep a wink last night.
        Although I tried with all my might.
        My thoughts were all of you.
Today, is Wednesday, what a day.
        It's taking hours to find its way.
        Wish it was gone, so I could say,
        Alas, good Thursday's here.
Today, is Thursday, three to go.
        Why am I glad? Why you should know.
        Soon your smiling face will show.
        Just thinking gives me cheer.
Today is Friday, bless this day.
        It's centuries since you've gone away,
        But soon you will return "Hooray".
        At last the weekends near
Watch Saturday and Sunday try
        To make all weekends tend to fly.
        And welcome back the week, too slow.
        Yeah, Monday, welcome dear.

FLICK OF AN EYELID

Life, though endless in the chronicles of time,

Is but a flick of an eyelid, in the span of mans'

existence.

While we are here, be happy that we have shared

this "flick of an eyelid" together.

UNTITLED

Bear with me, my heart, don't cry.

there was evil in his eye.

Hear the words I wish to say,

then begone, and let me stay.

FRIENDLY VOICE

I long for the sound of a friendly voice.

The sight of a face I love.

The touch of a hand,

The gaze in the eyes,

Of the only one I love.

MIND PAINTS

The mind paints such pretty pictures

which the heart believes, it seems.

But the eyes, all seeing, wise,

bring us back from tender dreams

TALL WHITE CANDLE

On the hushed alter of my heart

Where nobody can see,

A tall white candle stands apart,

And burns eternally.

This shining flame, I did not light,

But oh, there is no doubt.

Were I to strive, with all my might,

I could not blow it out.

UNTITLED

Are you all that I desire

and then some?

If my unworthy mind was so prone

to tell in magical phrase,

How would it say.....

I love you?

CALL TO PRAYER

The church spires that once called to prayer are silent now,

They reach up toward heaven, and wonder why and how

No one heeds their call, some think that God is irrelevant.

They feel they can do without him, only to find, they can't.

The call to prayer has never been so great.

Though some of us believe it never is too late.

Some wonder why God hasn't destroyed the world for all its sins.

And some believers pray that hopefully God soon wins.

So things will change for better, we pray that this we'll see.

If quite churches mean as much to you, as they do me.

Who can tell that now? It seems so hopeless in its loss.

How sad, for us, Gods son died upon the cross.

NE'ER FORGOTTEN

Sometimes we feel we're forgotten, and in a way, it's true.

For life takes on so many paths, with oh, so much to do.

That through a day, if some small thought, will flash across our mind,

To linger for a loving moment, a warming thought t find.

Then, if, right then we take the time to make a simple call,

It's possible you'll cheer a friend, if they are there at all.

To say "Can you believe I thought of you in such a pleasant way

that I just had to hear you, and what you have to say."

Or take the time to greet someone, who may be feeling low

in turn the day will give, to you, a very pleasant glow.

While we are now still able to, we will not soon forget,

We did our best to take the time, with nothing to regret.

EARLY YEARS OF CHRISTMAS MEMORIES

The snow begins to fall in feathered swirls around my head,
And I, a little girl again, remember times, now fled.
When drifts which once encompassed me, and seemed too big to climb,
Seem only little hillocks, now, there pictured in my mind

I, too recall at Christmas time, we'd clean the house and stair,
And polish all the furniture, to shirk, we wouldn't dare.
cause Santa clause was coming, to fill our lives with joys.
To spread beneath our Christmas tree, the many gifts and toys.
And then before he left the house he took a bag of stars,
To sprinkle tree and all beneath, including Danny's cars.

Then in the morning, Mamma would rise and light the tree a shine.
Then say that we could all come down oh, what a happy time.
The presents would be piled high our family was big
Too soon we'd have all gifts unwrapped as through the toys we'd dig
On Mom and Daddy we'd bestow our hugs and kisses too,
we knew who our sweet Santa's were, and that they loved us too.

For Linda there were dollies, and a bath to keep them clean
And Danny, little soldiers and real pin ball machine.
For Tommy one neat cowboy hat and a bright new bow and arrow
And Annie got a nice blue skirt which made her look quite narrow
And once when Daddy got new tires, we hid them in the shed
And filled a brand new garbage can with gifts all wrapped in red.
The ran a ribbon through the rooms beneath the tree to peek
So Mom and Daddy tracked the trail, their bigger gift to seek.
And Mamma always got some things to use within the house,
A waffle iron, a coffee pot, for her, a dress or blouse.
And I was not forgotten, I always got my share
of pretty colored packages all wrapped with loving care.

Then after that, the visiting when relatives would call,
they'd stand beneath the mistletoe for kisses one and all.

EARLY YEARS OF CHRISTMAS MEMORIES CONTINUED

Exchanging presents once again examining every toy.
Just seeing happiness and warmth, filled all our hearts with joy.

We nibbled goodies through the day, so dinner was forgot.
Besides pierogis filled the bill, reheated from the lot.
Then usually we'd be so tired from all the weeks preparing
That later in the twilight hours, just one thought we were sharing.
To climb between our fresh clean sheets and dream of such a day
When all we worked for, months on end, rewarded us this way.

And now, tradition lingers, so as the snowflakes fall,
My heart and mind go back in time, to happily recall.
So many Christmas mornings, and all the Christmas cheer.
To happily look forward to another one, this year.

BANANA SPLIT

Oh to taste the sweet honey of thee.

My hunger torments me and makes me weak.

Thou has shown me a small drop of thy delicacy

    yet has not allowed me to be fulfilled to my satisfaction.

I would devour thee tenderly so as not to harm thy precious beauty.

    then waiting for thy return, dream in anticipation.

SHORT THOUGHTS

I dreamed of you, and dreams were filled

    With tender song.

I felt that I did not belong.

    Too sweet the dream.

UNTITLED

A little ray of sunshine with every

    drop of rain.

A big or little error, with every

    human brain.

AND NOW GOODBYE

And I will be, like the the last page of a book you've read.

Warm in thought for some small while, and then,

forgotten.

Placed on the shelf of life to gather dust, in the memories

of your mind.

Sometimes, remembered, because of a familiar phrase or

melody.

Then, for a while, will the warmth return. Filling the void
with

me.

THE FOLLOWING PAGES ARE MORE POEMS...
WRITTEN BY MY BROTHER DANIEL R. KULIK.
(WRITING IS IN OUR BLOOD.)

No Love for Spring

Why do you cry, young spring?

    Your hair is filled with warm breezes,

    Yet your eyes are filled with tears.

    Does not the start of a new life bring

    joy instead of sorrow to your fresh awakening?

Why do you cry lovely spring?

    The scent of dormant life growing once again,

    fills the air with beautiful music,

    and your lips are kissed with soft, warm rain.

    Does this not ease, for a moment, your suffering?

Why do you cry, brave new spring?

    Winters 'cold treat has gone for a while

    And summer, with all this glory lies ahead.

    People will fall in love and begin to sing.

    But, you have no one to share with…this lovely happening.

Is that why you cry, lonely spring?

WHITE CLOUDS

White clouds float against a

    clear blue sky.

A warm wind carries the fragrant

    scent of a newly mowed lawn.

The coolness of green grass and

    the leaves of the trees,

make you want nothing more.......

    ....and nothing less.

THE SOMEONE TO TURN TO

The someone to turn to when
   fears fills your path,
The someone to guide you
   when dark is the night.

When blinded by diamonds,
   rubies and gems,
The someone to beat you
   for wanting of them.

The someone to cry with
   when sorrow is great.
The someone to laugh with cause
   there's nothing to hate.

When parting has come
   between Father and son,
There's no one to turn to,
   The long day is done.

SLOWLY

Slowly, I walked…. Each step faltering a little more than the previous one. This was my last mile. I never would be as carefree and gay as I had been before I did that unspeakable thing.

Why did I do it?

Then I thought of her, and remembered when we were kids, how we played together. Than later on, the dates. Well those were over now. They were such fun. I wonder where I went wrong. Why did it turn out this way? I take the final step…..and then I say

"I do".

LITTLE SISTERS

Little sisters, they aren't so bad.

Although they bug you and make you mad.

When you need a shirt for school,

her little steam iron is just the tool.

She has to get it good and hot,

a hole she burns, says she forgot.

Or when some friends drop in for cards,

her antics you cannot retard.

She'll throw a fit, she'll start a fight.

I'll yell at her with all my might,

but it's no use, she still is there,

Her smiles turn oaths into a prayer.

For I have one thing left to do

and that I find is always true.

To love her now while still can,

else I must wait till years do span.

For she will grow, and me, heart sore,

she will not pester anymore.

"Conscience can be man's most intimate friend,
yet his most personal enemy."

God's Pencil

People who fear death greatly
            have only one thing left.
      To pray to live forever,
          for fear of death, is death.

God's Pencil

Each time my pen writes "deceased" after
                    my Father's name, it cries.

HAVE BUS - WILL WALK

The first thing, a 2 -4- 5
I raise my voice in cheer
But when I see the NFT
I'm filled with crushing fear.

The first bus is too crowded,
The second will be less!
I kid myself, "I get a seat?"
The sign reads 'S O S"

I wait until the third one,
It surely can't be more.
Oh, yes it is, it's just my luck
It's crammed from door to door.

But finally comes an empty bus
at last I'll get some rest.
And though I'm here, it goes right by,
I'll walk............. it's easiest.